Praises for *Make Lemonade*

"Donna D does more than gently charm you with good writing. She causes you to consider that you have the power to be a changemaker. Make Lemonade is a book of fiction that could be the cure to all social injustice in the world. It is a book of reflection that causes the reader to come back into the reality that all humanity needs is someone to care. Could that someone be you?"

Bishop Rick Thomas
Abundant Life Christian Center, Margate, Florida

"*Make Lemonade* uncovers an uncomfortable dilemma in our society. It is easy for many prosperous adults to turn a blind eye to the reality of displaced and suffering children. This story mirrors that of many whose hearts have softened to the plight of the most vulnerable members of our society. I pray it will open many eyes and hearts to the children."

Mary Perdue
Former First Lady of Georgia, Wife of Governor Sonny Perdue

"Our lives are a tapestry. Most of the time we see the underside—the knots and broken ends, a myriad of seemingly unrelated pieces. Yet sometimes we see a glimpse on top and things start to make sense. An intricately designed masterpiece is being woven for each of us. Donna D captures the marvel of the tapestry with her marvelous storytelling in this book, *Make Lemonade*. As the mother of three precious gifts from God through adoption, I highly recommend you read the book and anything else Donna D writes."

Jennifer Kemp Andrews
Daughter of Congressman Jack Kemp, GOP Vice Presidential Nominee

"*Make Lemonade* is a sweet tale of a sophisticated, self-centered millionaire whose selfish ambitions land her in a precarious brush with reality. Her disdain for children and the elderly suddenly changes as she encounters an unsuspecting ordeal that gives her a true taste of love in the most unusual way. This charming story will inspire and captivate you from beginning to end."

Eric Lige
Singer/ Songwriter/ Vocal Coach/ Producer
Worship Leader, Saddleback Church

"*Make Lemonade* has been a labor of love for Donna D. Every element, including the up close and personal encounter with the foster care and adoption system, is purposed with her ever-present love for the wee ones. *Make Lemonade* will make you laugh and make you cry, but most importantly it will touch your heart."

Michele Clark Jenkins
Author & Co-Founder, Sisters in Faith

"Only someone who knows first-hand how to make lemonade out of lemons could write such a beautiful story of love and redemption, and do it with both heart and humor. Do yourself a favor and read this book. Donna D can tell a story like nobody I know."

Kimberley Kennedy
News Anchor, ABC
Speaker/ Author of Left at the Altar

"*Make Lemonade* details the life interrupted of self-made millionaire, music mogul Casey Alliston. Donna D's characters are complex, real and raw and the storyline is peppered with equal parts of tenderness and humor. With all of its twists and turns, you'll feel like you're riding shotgun on this road trip to redemption. I would read anything she writes."

Jan Smith (Mama Jan)
Producer/ writer/ singer/ vocal coach
Speaker/ author of Run the Other Way

"Through the heartwarming and magnetic story of *Make Lemonade* you'll be inspired to turn your obstacles into steppingstones and your pain into gain."

Dr. Helen Delaney
International Speaker
Chaplin for American Caribbean Experience Ministry
Co-contributor for Sisters in Faith Holy Bible

"Donna D is a homespun real-life storyteller. The characters in *Make Lemonade* step out of each page to move your own heart and leave you thirsty for more. This would make a wonderful must-see family television series or movie!"

Dorothy Ellington
Donna D's 4th grade teacher, friend and prayer partner

"Casey Alliston had it all until her aggressive attitude causes unexpected problems and her life seems to be crumbling. Two hundred hours of community service reveals a vulnerability she was not aware of. Her story is told with sensitivity and sensibility insisting even amidst life's most difficult challenges, the happy ending is still a possibility."

Joseph Litsch
Emmy-Award winning set decorator
Contributor/ Hallmark Hall of Fame Museum

"A bright, refreshing and poignant story of the power of love, *Make Lemonade* reminds us of how life's most painful situations can turn out to be the sweetest of all when love is in the mix. Taking the bitter with the sweet is often the best recipe for helping us to open our hearts to love and forgiveness—to put the past behind us and embrace what lies ahead. No one knows this better than Donna D, my dear friend and one of the finest writers I know. She has a way of writing the story of all of our lives."

Babbie Mason
Award-winning Singer-Songwriter and Author
www.babbie.com

Make Lemonade

by Donna I. Douglas Walchle

This book is a work of fiction. Names, characters, businesses, organizations, places, events, and incidents either are the product of the author's imagination or are used fictitiously. Any resemblance to actual persons, living or dead, events, or locales is entirely coincidental.

Copyright © 2013 by Donna Douglas, Inc.

All rights reserved.

Published in the United States by Donna D Here Publishing, a division of Donna Douglas Inc., Atlanta, Georgia.

www.donnadhere.com

Jacket design by Dorian Straszewski/ www.abysmalblue.com

Jacket photographs © Tara Amos/ Tara Amos Photography

Library of Congress Cataloging-in-Publication Data is on file with the Library of Congress.

ISBN: 978-0-9891123-0-7

Dedication

To all of the special people in this world who open their heart and their home to make a difference in the life of a child. Thank you for demonstrating what real love is and what a loving family looks like. I am certain that every time an adoption occurs and every time a foster child is embraced, that God smiles and that all of heaven applauds. *Make Lemonade* is dedicated to all of you!

DONNA I. DOUGLAS WALCHLE

MAKE LEMONADE

Chapter 1

It is predawn and still pitch black outside as the alarm clock sounds off. Casey Alliston, the youthful, late-thirties founder and president of Hit Maker Music, sluggishly emerges from underneath a mound of covers and slaps the blaring annoyance into silent submission. She stares in utter disbelief, as she seems to every day, at the red numbers revealing it's 5:30 a.m. Slowly she frees her way from under the covers, stands upright and makes her way to the bathroom.

Almost as though in a trance, she re-enters the bedroom wearing her sweatsuit and Reebocks. She opens her wall-to-wall curtains, hits play on her preselected music library of iPod favorites and makes her way to the stationary bike in the corner of her expansive Midtown penthouse suite. Very quickly she comes alive and, as with everything else in her life, rides with tenacious determination as if the only goal is to win.

Her bedroom walls are lined with awards and photographs with celebrities and political figures, all of whom echo her philosophy: *If you're going to be in the game, be at the top of it.* Apart from recognition and success, there is no other point.

The sun begins to rise, painting slivers of peach, purple and orange hues across the horizon. She gazes out at the skyline and admires The Hit Maker Music high rise prominently displayed in the distance. After an hour of cardio, she hits the shower.

Dressed chicly, with flawless hair and perfectly applied makeup, she steps out of the elevator forty floors below, into the poshly decorated lobby. The building manager, holding a USA Today newspaper, greets her.

"Good morning, Ms. Alliston."

Intercepting the newspaper, she responds, "Mr. Mason, how are you this morning?"

"Fine, thank you. I see your artist, Erika Marie, has another #1 hit on her hands."

"How about that," she responds as she winks and exits through the door being held open for her by a doorman.

Freshly washed, waxed and awaiting her entrance, her bright red vintage T-bird convertible with the license tag *HITMKR* is parked at the curb with the driver's door open. She assumes the pilot's seat and cautiously exits the driveway into early-morning Atlanta traffic. She cranks up the stereo just shy of potential inner-ear injury. It's how she likes her music and it's how she lives her life. Unapologetically out loud.

The fifteen-minute drive to work always flies by. But when the DJ announces that Erika Marie's song, "The Hard Way," has topped the Billboard charts at #1, Casey wishes this ride would shift into slow motion. *How timely,* she thought, that she'd be in the car to hear her latest success story being announced to the entire world!

As the song ends she pulls into valet parking, with her usual perfect timing. She quickly exits and briskly walks into her building: her world, the one where she is the queen, the ruler, the winner and still the champion.

The elevator door opens and Casey is met by Annie, her preppy, twenty-something assistant. Holding a clipboard in one hand, Annie passes off a Starbucks triple latte to Casey with her other hand, a smooth routine she could perform in her sleep. She follows Casey down the hall toward the conference room and reels off questions requiring Casey's approval.

"Bud Marie called this morning and wants an advance on Erika Marie's travel budget."

"Manager-parents! A breed all their own. Fine. Have Bert cut a check and I'll sign it."

"And Winnie called and asked if you could have lunch today?"

"Of course I can have lunch with my bestie, Wins. Call her back and ask her if we can do one o' clock at Grecco's."

As Casey flings open the conference room door a loud, unified chorus of a dozen enthusiastic employees chants, "We're number one! We're number one!"

Casey smiles approvingly. The conference room overflows with Hit Maker Music memorabilia. Posters and photos from Hit Maker Music's numerous top-selling artists adorn the walls. Community sponsor commendations are plentiful and proudly displayed: *The Integrity Award, Just Say No to Drugs, Friends Don't Let Friends Drive Drunk,* and *Character in the Schools Tour* commendations line the sideboard. The numerous gold and multi-platinum CD's could serve as wallpaper.

As the cheering fades, everyone begins to applaud. Casey gives a thumbs up and motions everyone to take a seat. Casey is brief on acknowledgments and is not known for living in the moment. She always challenges herself and others to push forward, on to the next goal. Her comments are short.

"You all had a part in this most recent success. You should be proud of yourselves. Thank you for all of your hard work and effort. Now let's get down to the business at hand."

Casey directs her first question to Jack, a thirty-year-old marketing manager who's been with the company for three years. He's hard-working, creative and delivers with style and timeliness. But he would step on his mother's back to climb the corporate ladder. Casey trusts his credentials but doesn't trust him.

"Jack, how's the sponsorship package coming for Erika Marie's tour?"

"It's all locked down, Casey. I offered them the same package as last year and they jumped at it!"

"Same as last year? The exposure we're bringing them is tremendous!"

"But they came on board with us when Erika Marie was still an unknown."

Slightly annoyed, Casey responds, "But she's no longer unknown, Jack. That's the point! You'll need to pull in another sponsor."

"But the tour is in three weeks," Jack retorts.

Casey raises her eyebrow, awaiting an appropriate response.

"I'll get right on it," Jack offers in a tone of resistant compliance peppered with an immense helping of ego deflation.

Casey moves on to acknowledge the raised hand of Bert Elliot: the immaculately dressed, silver-haired, sixty-four year-old voice of reason who serves as her COO.

"Yes, Bert?"

"Casey, the gospel music scene is exploding. I move that we explore the potential of expanding our roster. We've got to drill where there is oil and this looks like a major money maker!"

Jack lifts both hands and begins waving them as he shouts, "I second it!"

Casey gives Jack a look of distain and then turns back to Bert with an emphatic, "Motion denied! Bert, you're our *money* man. We count of you to keep our figures straight, not to be creative." She smiles wryly and continues, "Am I not giving you enough to do?"

Everyone quietly observes this intensely close tennis match. Bert makes a second attempt to convince her.

"Casey, this matter needs due consideration. Read Billboard! Gospel music is the fastest growing genre in the world today! I know how you feel about religion. But this has nothing to do with religion. It has to do with our bottom line. I'm telling you that gospel music is a cash cow!"

"And I'm telling you, Bert, that it's not for us! I have no interest in gospel music! Anything else?"

An uncomfortable silence envelops the conference room. Many of the employees squirm, avoid eye contact and attempt to appear as though they are taking comprehensive notes on their laptops. Embarrassed and angered by Casey's response, Bert manages to hold his tongue, although his crimson-color cheeks expose a gasket close to blowing.

Annie, in her always-positive cheerleader fashion, ignores the atmosphere and offers an upbeat announcement. Delivered with true team motivational skills and falling just short of waving multi-color pompoms, she announces, "Remember we're all expected at the NARAS Awards banquet on Saturday!"

Casey chimes in, "Cocktails at my place beforehand!"

Casey begins to applaud and everyone follows suit.

"Good job everyone! You're dismissed."

They stand and exit except for Casey and Bert, who closes the door behind them and waits for Casey to finish up her notes. Jack, noticing that Bert has stayed behind to speak with Casey privately, rushes into his office and turns on the intercom, hoping to eavesdrop.

Bert addresses her in stern and pointed tones.

"Casey, I didn't like the way you minimized my value by slamming my suggestion. You seem to forget that I'm the one who gave you the seed capital to start this company."

Three doors away, Jack listens with great satisfaction and relishes the correction he only wishes he could impart.

Without looking up from what she is typing she replies, unmoved and in monotone, "Bert, c'mon. You've gotten your investment back a gazillion times over."

Bert fires back, "I was wealthy when we met. My return is not the point. You were disrespectful."

For a long pause, Casey pensively stares at her laptop screen.

"Bert I apologize if I stepped on your ego, but you have never been a part of the creative decisions around here. I have always called all the shots. What would make today any different? Stay in your lane!"

She shakes her head, gathers her belongings, stands and exits; leaving Bert alone in the conference room with no closure.

Sure that there is an electric short somewhere with his equipment, Jack checks the plugs on his intercom. He cannot imagine that Casey has failed to spar. But he is certain of this: there is a dent in the armor. And he intends to use it as another rung on his climb to the top. He can work on Bert. He will work with Bert. Bert deserved to have his ideas supported. After all, for as long as Jack can remember, one of his greatest assets had always been to divide and conquer.

Chapter 2

Grecco's Italian restaurant has been a favorite of Casey and her best friend, Winnie Jenkins, a mild-mannered, African-American public defender, since they graduated from college. It is here they have celebrated and mourned all the good, the bad and the ugly occasions of their lives. From the slightly cracked red-leather booths, to the black and white 8x10 autographed celebrity photos lining the walls, to the moving and rich sounds of Nessun Dorma, to a great wine list and exceptional food, this place has felt like home to them for close to twenty years.

It's 1:35 p.m. Winnie sits alone at a corner booth, nibbling on breadsticks and reading legal briefs as Casey flies through the door.

"Sorry I'm running late, Wins!"

Winnie smiles, stands to give her a hug and says playfully, "Casey, you've been running late for the last twenty years!"

Smiling, Casey slightly shoves her, sits down and places her napkin in her lap.

"Well at least I came with major news!"

Pretending not to know her news, Winnie attempts to look curious.

"'The Hard Way' went to #1!"

Breaking into a wide smile, Winnie offers, "Congratulations! I'm surprised your head could fit through the door!"

The two have a good laugh as the waiter exchanges the breadsticks basket for a basket of Greccos' signature hot garlic rolls.

Ruth Bayslow, a late-sixties socialite carrying a large purse with a teacup poodle peeking out of the top of it, approaches their table. Casey and Winnie both stand to greet her.

"Hello, Casey," Ruth exclaims in a slow southern drawl. "I saw your interview on GMA yesterday, dahlin'. You were beyond fabulous!"

"Thanks, Ruth. Ruth, this is my longtime and best friend, Winnie Jenkins, attorney at law."

"How do you do, Winnie. A pleasure to meet you."

"Winnie, this is Ruth Bayslow. Ruth is on the Board of Directors for Hit Maker Music."

"The pleasure is mine. Nice to meet you, as well."

"Well, I'm off to tea at the Ritz. Casey, I really want you to meet my son, the widower. I think you'd get on grandly!"

Reserved, but politely, Casey responds, "Yes, we'll try to do that sometime."

"Very well then, ta ta, ladies! Enjoy your lunch!"

Ruth moves toward the door and just before she exits her concealed dog lets out several shrieking yelps. Obviously busted, Ruth hurries out the revolving door before the management tries to restrain her. Casey and Winnie resume their conversation as Casey peruses the menu.

"Casey, you should meet the widower!"

"When? Between two and four a.m., when I have nothing better to do?"

Winnie smirks at her and then excitedly professes, "Well, you're not the only one with news today. I have some of my own."

Casey stops reading the menu, all ears and poised for the announcement.

"Well, spill it, girlie! Don't keep me in suspense!"

"Okay, I met someone."

"What? No way! That's great! Who is he?"

"His name is Dominic. I met him at church. He also volunteers at the Eagle's Nest with me."

"That is awesome, Wins! Tell me more!"

"Nothing more to tell you yet except that he seems to have a lot of great qualities and is a total hunk! But I'll keep you posted as events unfold."

"This is so exciting for you! Can't wait to meet him."

As though she doesn't know it by heart, Casey glances back over the menu.

"So what are you having for lunch today, Winnie?"

"You want to split a Caesar salad and each have a side of pasta?"

"Perfect!"

As if on cue, the waiter approaches the table carrying a tray with a large Caesar salad and two sides of pasta.

"Good," Winnie says with complete confidence. "Because that's what I ordered for us twenty minutes before your tardy butt showed up!"

The waiter stands at attention holding a fresh block of parmigiano reggiano and a cheese grater.

"Some fresh cheese, ladies?"

As though rehearsed, in concert they respond, "Yes, please!"

After lunch, they do what they always do on a sunny, clear day. They continue talking and walk arm-in-arm through the streets of Midtown. As they round a busy corner, a young homeless woman in her early twenties with tangled hair, soiled clothes and in need of a bath, catches Winnie's attention. Casey knows what comes next. She's seen this tender heart in action time and time again. Winnie's stride comes to a halt.

"Rachael?"

The young girl stops, turns and then makes her way over to them.

"Rachael, you know you can go to the shelter?"

"Yeah, I know," Rachael replies quietly.

Winnie opens her purse, pulls out some change and hands it to her. Tears well up in Rachael's eyes. She hugs Winnie before remembering she is dirty and smelly and should keep her distance. She tries to brush off Winnie's shoulder. Winnie takes her hand and looks into her eyes.

"It's okay to need help. The shelter can help you."

Sheepishly, Rachael looks at her and nods, acknowledging Winnie's advice. She turns and walks away in the opposite direction. Winnie watches her until she disappears around the first corner.

"I can't believe you call *these people* by name. I hope you don't tell them where you live."

"*These people* are my clients. And she's not dangerous, she's homeless."

"Well if you ever get tired of being Joan of Arc Junior, you can come to work for me, you know."

"Casey, you know I love my job, but since you're feeling so generous today there is something I wanted to talk with you about."

"Okay, what?"

"I'd appreciate you taking a meeting with a good friend of mine, Phyllis Early."

"Does she want a record deal?"

"Does your mind ever go anywhere else? No she does not want a record deal."

Casey, perplexed, stares in utter cluelessness as she awaits the next hint.

"Phyllis Early heads the Eagle's Nest where I volunteer. I've told you about it. They house orphans, foster children and senior citizens."

"Winnie, you know how I feel about handouts. People have to take responsibility for their station in life!"

"Casey, these are children and senior citizens."

"My point exactly! Where are the parents of the children and where are the children of the old people?"

"Casey, sometimes you are so myopic. Have you ever thought about the fact that maybe God has allowed your success so that you can help a few of those who are less fortunate?"

"*Allowed* my success? God, if there even is a God, hasn't done a thing for me. I've worked my butt off to get where I am!"

"Casey, Phyllis has the *teach-them-to-fish* rather than *give-them-a-fish* philosophy. Just take the meeting. If you still feel the same way afterwards, then fine."

Casey shakes her head and surrenders to the inevitable.

"Okay, have her call me."

"Phyllis will be at your office today at 4:00 p.m."

"Today? But I'm busy today. I'm sure I don't have any time on this short of notice."

"I already spoke with Annie. You know Annie, your assistant who keeps your schedule? And apparently you have the time, Missy."

Casey rolls her eyes, gives Winnie a hug and mutters, "It's a conspiracy."

And so, the deal was sealed just as they arrived at the corner of *you go your way, I go mine*. Winnie continues to walk west and Casey heads south, back to Hit Maker Music to await her 4 p.m. appointment. Winnie rests another case.

Chapter 3

Casey's office is her home away from home, her second sanctuary. It would be difficult to find even one square inch in this spacious, lavishly decorated space that doesn't boast of her plethora of successes. Platinum records, bronze plaques, framed pictures of society events, even a *Woman of the Year* award, all point to the many accomplishments of this self-made millionaire.

Her only hobbies are photography and watercolor painting. Her subjects are landscapes, seascapes and flowers, rather than people. Places and objects are beautiful, yet controllable. People, not so much. Her pieces are beautifully framed and displayed in true art-gallery form, including perfectly placed pin lighting all along her east wall.

It's 4 p.m. and Phyllis Early, late-fifties, well-dressed, prim and proper, sits across from Casey and begins her pitch.

"Thank you for seeing me, Ms. Alliston."

Casey is direct and quickly goes to the bottom line. Time is money. In this meeting she sees no wrung to boost her higher on the ladder. For that matter, she sees no ladder at all.

"Mrs. Early, let me be brutally honest with you. Writing a check or starting a program to cure social ills is far from my philosophy."

"Winnie mentioned that. But I thought if perhaps you could get to know some of our residents personally, that ..."

Irritated at the very thought, Casey interrupts.

"Mrs. Early."

Insistent and refusing to be so quickly defeated, Phyllis tries another angle.

"If not a contribution then, would you ever consider volunteering? Perhaps teaching a music class? Or, Winnie says that you're a wonderful photographer and quite the artist."

"Mrs. Early, I don't have time to see my own friends as much as I'd like, much less ..."

Phyllis is unmoved and not in the least bit discouraged as she points to Casey's collection of photography and watercolors.

"Is this some of your work?"

"Yes."

"Our residents love when someone comes to teach a special class. They have so little in life."

"Mrs. Early, I just don't have the time or the desire to be a part of anything like that," Casey responds matter-of-factly. "Is there anything else?"

Realizing that at least for today she is getting nowhere fast, Phyllis stands and extends her hand. Casey rises to meet her and shakes her hand. Phyllis addresses her with determination and faith.

"Thank you for seeing me, Ms. Alliston. It was a pleasure to meet you. I'm going to continue praying for you and all of the possibilities that God might place on your heart."

"God, if there even is a God …"

"Oh, there is. I hope to see you again soon, Ms. Alliston. Have a good afternoon."

Casey watches her leave the office and then glances at her wall of art and photos. She sits back down and swivels around to face the Atlanta skyline. Annie enters, interrupting her contemplation.

"The caterer just called to confirm that they will be there with the hors d' oeuvres at 5:00 p.m. And the florist will deliver the centerpiece you ordered at the same time."

"Perfect! It's going to be a great night."

※ ※ ※

Every year Casey looks forward to the National Academy of Recording Arts and Sciences Awards Banquet. This year even more so, because she is being honored as an industry leader and will receive the Integrity Award. This award is especially meaningful to her because it spotlights her initiative insisting on a drug-free environment for her workplace, as well as for all of her artists on tour. Her singular purpose is having a positive influence on the youth who follow and support her artists. Casey wants her roster to be exemplary role models.

To set the tone, she has planned the perfect pre-celebration gathering at her penthouse condominium for all the employees and associates at Hit Maker Music. The menu will be smoked salmon with dill sauce on toast points, grilled shrimp cocktail, mushrooms stuffed with crabmeat, artichoke dip with sourdough bread, and assorted cheeses with fruit, served with vintage white and red wines. Of course there will be toasting to their success. And toasting is not possible without perfectly chilled Dom Perignon.

At 6 p.m. Casey's doorman announces her guests. Dressed in an Armani evening gown, Casey greets them at the door. Bert, Jack, Annie, Erika Marie and her dad, Bud, and a dozen others file in. Several waiters dressed in tuxedos and white gloves take coats and hats from her guests. Others begin making their rounds with trays of food and wine. Casey stands back and observes as she sips sparkling water. She enjoys watching a superbly executed plan unfold. And this one is.

After a respectable time of socializing, Casey leads her guests into her dining room. A rosewood table holds an elegant centerpiece of calla lilies posed in a Waterford crystal vase. Fluted champagne glasses surround the vase in semi-circular formation. Two waiters remove the bottles of Dom Perignon chilling in sterling silver wine buckets, pop their corks and pour. Everyone politely holds a glass awaiting their hostess's proposal. Casey raises her glass.

"Here's to Hit Maker Music and the best staff and artists on the planet!"

Everyone raises a glass and enjoys the bubbly. The waiter pours Casey a second glass that she quickly consumes.

"Now let's all head downstairs to our limos. We have designated drivers, so no worries."

Casey moves toward the front door, opens it and methodically ushers everyone out. Bert lingers behind and holds up his wine glass, signaling a waiter for a refill. Feeling no pain, Bert takes the bottle from the waiter. Balancing his full glass and the bottle he makes his way toward the door where Casey stands waiting so she can lock up. Just as he gets to Casey, one of the waiters summons him.

"Excuse me sir, I think you left your scarf."

As Bert awkwardly turns to retrieve his scarf, his wine glass brushes Casey's shoulder, spilling wine down the front of her gown. Casey quickly grabs a linen napkin and tries to wipe off the spill.

"Oh no, Casey, look what I've done. I am so sorry."

"It was an accident. What's done is done. You go ahead with everyone else. I'll change and meet you there."

Casey hurriedly goes to her closet and pulls out another of her many designer fashions. She changes out her purse, jewelry and shoes. The limos have taken the others and she will have to drive herself. She is already running late and has not a second to spare. After all, it would be rude to be late for an event where she is the one being honored. She picks up her phone to the concierge.

"Yes, good evening. Please bring my car around. And please hurry. I'm on my way down and I'm running late for an event."

🎵🎵🎵

The Four Seasons Hotel is one of the finest in Atlanta. Limos line the driveway in double file as producers, songwriters, celebrities and music industry execs emerge to the perpetual pelting of consecutive camera flashes and a press core hungry for interviews.

The ballroom is elegantly decorated and a string quartet plays classical music. An NARAS banner cascades over the front of the head table. A larger banner serves as a backdrop on the stage. A massive mahogany podium sits front and center. The dining tables are formally set with fine linen, silver, crystal and china. The wait staff carries silver serving platters of scrumptious lobster dinners for all the guests.

🎵🎵🎵

Casey pulls out of her driveway and accelerates down Peachtree Street. After making an illegal U-turn she runs a red light just as she hears a siren and looks in her rearview mirror to see flashing blue lights.

"This is not happening!"

Since she is within a couple of blocks of the Four Seasons she decides not to pull over, but to speed up. She will convince the officer of her innocence when she arrives.

The officer calls in for assistance. "Unit 12 on Peachtree turning west onto 14th Street pursuing a vintage Thunderbird, license *HITMKR*. Driver resisting. Request backup."

※ ※ ※

The star power in the ballroom is immense. The Hit Maker Music staff is in place, all in a celebratory mood, but for the empty seat awaiting Casey, the woman of the hour. The ballroom seems unusually chilly to be so heavily occupied. Bert is unfazed and toasts everyone and everything but the chandelier. Not insulated by alcohol consumption, Annie shivers and realizes she is missing her wrap.

"I'm freezing! I left my wrap in the limo. I'll be right back. I hope Casey's pulling up by now."

Jack stands up and offers assistance.

"Annie, I'll get your wrap. And I'll look for Casey while I'm outside. I want to have a puff or two of my cigar."

Jack walks outside just as Casey pulls into the Four Seasons Hotel driveway, trailed by three police cars, all with lights flashing. Jack pauses just outside the entrance doors, lights up a cigar and stares in amused disbelief.

Somewhat irritated, somewhat humiliated, Casey looks in her rear view mirror, and says with complete indignation, "What a trio of idiots! This is what my tax dollars go for? Unbelievable!"

Casey steps out of her car as Nick Patroni, a local policeman in his early forties, approaches her. Jack begins to video the event with his cell phone.

"Officer, shouldn't you be making better use of your time?" Casey fires off sarcastically. "I'm late for an awards banquet inside, an awards banquet where I am being honored. Look, I know I was speeding. Just write me a ticket and leave it on the dash." She begins walking away.

"Ma'am, I need to see your driver's license, registration and proof of insurance."

Nick turns to the other officers, telling them that he can handle things and they can go.

Agitated and close to the boiling point, Casey gets back into her car and rummages around in the glove box for her registration and proof of insurance. She hands them to Nick and searches her purse for her license.

"Ms. Alliston, your registration and insurance have lapsed?"

"What! That's not possible. Well, I probably have the current ones at my office. Just haven't had a chance to put them in my car yet."

"Ma'am, it's illegal to operate a motor vehicle without it being registered and insured."

"Yeah, yeah, I'm aware. Well, write me up for that, too. Did I mention I'm late for an awards banquet that's honoring me?"

"You did, twice now. Can I see your license, please?"

Casey replies sternly, "Look, Officer, I changed purses and forgot my license. I was supposed to be transported by limo until one of my employees spilled wine on me at a pre-celebration party we were having at my home. I had to stay behind to change clothes and then I drove myself."

A crowd has gathered. Several people eavesdrop on the conversation. One couple looks at their *In Style Magazine* and realizes the face on the cover is the same as the woman who is being reprimanded by the police. Numerous paparazzi begin taking pictures. Jack places a call on his cell phone.

"News desk, how may I help you?"

Jack speaks quietly into his cell, "Yes, I'd like to give you an anonymous tip."

Nick begins writing Casey a ticket.

"In addition to driving without a license, an expired registration and no proof of insurance, you ran a red light, made an illegal U-turn and resisted arrest."

Jack approaches the scene and should win an Oscar for his sincere offer of help. "Casey, I don't know what's going on but this looks horrible. I'll go inside and get Bert. He can call your attorney."

Completely ignoring Jack's offer, Casey resumes her rant.

"Look, this is ridiculous, Officer! My name is Casey Alliston. By chance did you watch *Good Morning America* on Thursday? I was a guest! I'm on the covers of *Time Magazine, In Style Magazine* and *People Magazine,* all in the same month."

Casey follows Nick to his car and continues to argue her case.

Bert steps outside the hotel with Jack in tow, observes all the commotion and makes his way through the crowd toward Casey.

"Officer, what's going on here?" Bert slurs, permeating the air with the strong scent of alcohol.

Casey reads the officer's name tag.

"Bert, tell this Nick Patroni who I am."

"Officer, this is Casey Alliston, the President of Hit Maker Music. I accidentally spilled wine on her and she had to change clothes. The rest of our party came ahead in limos."

Thinking he was making big points with Officer Patroni he further mentions, "We always hire limos so we have a designated driver."

"Were you drinking, Ms. Alliston?"

"I proposed a toast or two. So, collectively maybe a glass? Actually, I don't normally drink at all," Casey states emphatically.

Nick reaches into his car and pulls out a Breathalyzer.

"I'll need you to blow into this, Ma'am."

"I'm not blowing into that!"

"Ms. Alliston, we can do this here or down at the station."

The crowd of onlookers grows and cameras flash repeatedly. A limo carrying Ruth Bayslow and several of her guests pulls up to the curb. Ruth, formally dressed, exits the limo with her teacup poodle peering out of her large, sequined purse.

As she and her guests walk toward the hotel entrance, one of her guests exclaims, "Ruth, isn't that your friend, Casey Alliston, blowing into a Breathalyzer?"

Ruth looks over at Casey but pretends not to recognize her.

"It's too dark to tell, but I'm certain it's not."

Nick reads the results of the Breathalyzer.

"Ma'am, I'm placing you under arrest."

Casey interrupts, "Oh hell no, you're not!"

Jack presses *record* on his phone. Bert appears to sober up a little, and is dumbfounded.

"For DUI, speeding, running a red light, making an illegal U-turn, driving without a license, resisting arrest and no proof of insurance or registration."

Nick turns Casey around and attempts to handcuff her.

Casey jerks her arm away from him and gets in his face.

"DUI! Look, Patroni, you are making a huge mistake. How can I be drunk? I had a couple of toasts! I don't even drink!"

Nick ignores her, puts the cuffs on her and eases her into the backseat of the patrol car as cameras go on flashing.

Casey continues in protest, "Listen to me! My taxes pay your salary! You overzealous, self-righteous … You should be out arresting criminals! I will have your badge!"

A tow truck arrives and begins hooking up Casey's T-Bird to remove it from the Four Seasons driveway. From the rear window of the police car, Casey's expression is one of shock and disbelief as she exchanges looks of hopelessness with Bert.

The police car pulls out of the driveway and onto 14th Street, with blue lights flashing. They head downtown where Casey will be formally charged as a first-time offender for multiple counts of breaking the law.

Chapter 4

Officer Patroni escorts Casey, handcuffs and all, inside the station to a processing window. The woman officer in charge is chewing a large wad of gum. Her hair looks like a red swirl of straw-like meringue piled high atop her head. She relieves Casey of all of her possessions and signs her in.

"I need to make a call. I get one call, don't I?"

"Sure honey, you can make your call. But we have to book you first."

Next comes a claustrophobic room permeated with the stale scent of old cigarette butts where they un-cuff her, drag her index finger and thumb onto a pad soaked with black ink and press each firmly on a cardboard card. Finally they stand her against a blank wall lined with a measuring tape indicating her height is 5'5". They take mug shots from various angles.

Indignantly Casey asks, "Now can I make my one phone call?"

Casey is escorted to a pay phone not requiring coins where she calls Winnie. She is both infuriated and scared to death. Her voice is trembling.

"Winifred, it's Casey, where are you? You're not going to believe this, because I sure don't! I have been arrested and I'm in the county jail. Please come and bail me out as soon as you get this! Hurry, Winnie. This is a nightmare!"

This entire evening seems as surreal as it gets. That is, until Officer Wilma Perdue, Casey's jailer for the night, leads her to a large, heavy, barred iron door. Officer Perdue opens it with a key that is securely attached to her thick black belt loop. They go inside. Casey flanks Officer Perdue down a long hallway of full cells where whistles and jeers are commonplace. When they reach the end of the corridor, Officer Perdue unlocks Casey's holding cell and motions with her head for Casey to enter. She complies. Officer Perdue slams the door behind her and locks it.

The cell has several typical Friday-night occupants. Sparsely clad hookers talk amongst themselves and a tattooed neo-Nazi type occupies a top bunk. Harmony Jones, a large African-American woman in her mid-forties, wearing glasses as thick as Coke bottles and sporting a 70's hair do and braces, snores loudly from an adjacent bunk. Rachael, the young homeless woman who is a client of Winnie's, sits on a bottom bunk watching Casey pace like a caged animal. Slowly Rachael stands and musters the nerve to approach Casey.

"Excuse me?"

Casey looks at her but keeps pacing. Suddenly, Harmony ceases snoring from the top bunk and begins stretching and stirring about.

"Isn't your name Casey?" Rachael asks.

"Great," Casey responds sarcastically. "How'd you know that? Did you see me on *Good Morning America* or on the cover of a magazine at a newsstand?"

"Ah, I don't know anything about that. Aren't you Winnie's friend? I met you one day on the street when you were walking with Winnie. She gave me money. Do you remember?"

Rachel extends her hand to Casey, but Casey does not reciprocate.

"I'm Rachael. Winnie's my friend, too."

Casey stops pacing and whispers firmly, "Winnie's not your friend. She's your attorney or your caseworker, but she's not your friend!"

Rachael ignores her rudeness.

"She's going to be upset with me. I got pulled in again for loitering."

Harmony listens in on the conversation and weighs in.

"You and Winnie friends?"

"Oh geez, what is this, ole' home week for every client Winnie has? Look, Winnie is my friend. You do not know her on the same level as I do."

"Oh, but I'm sure I do! I'm the choir director at her church," Harmony debates.

Completely disgusted, Casey continues to pace and mumble to herself.

"Homeless people, church people … what a freakin' nightmare!"

Harmony begins to pace alongside Casey.

"Winnie's on her way to spring us right now. Rachael and I were arrested when we got a little rowdy during a protest for the homeless. They charged us with loitering. What crime did you commit?"

"I didn't do anything that warrants being arrested!"

Everyone in the cells laughs and shakes their heads. Harmony tries to be the voice of reason.

"Must be your first time in the slammer, huh? I remember my first time. Denial is your best friend. But you know what, baby, the sooner you can admit that you're in here because you broke the law, the better off you'll be. You'll get there. One way or the other, I assure you: you'll get there."

Casey, completely insulted that she is being advised by a church person, resumes pacing without comment.

Officer Perdue approaches the cell and makes an announcement.

"Casey Alliston, Rachael Austin and Harmony Jones, your bail has been posted."

"It's about damn time," Casey states as she butts in front of the others to secure her first place position getting out of the cell.

It's midnight and the mood is somber as Casey, Winnie, Rachael and Harmony walk slowly down the stone steps of the police station.

"Wins, the manner in which I was treated was inexcusable! When I finish with that officer he'll be lucky to be reading parking meters!" Casey shouts.

"Casey, lower your voice."

Harmony chimes in.

"Yeah girl, don't be disturbing the peace. They'll toss you right back in the slammer-roony."

Casey comes to a complete halt, extends her arms in a motion indicating to stop and without any eye contact to Harmony, addresses Winnie.

"Pardon me. Not to be rude, but Winnie, I have been traumatized. I have been through a lot tonight. And I really need to speak with you privately, not in front of these people I do not know."

With that, Casey turns her back to the others and crosses her arms. With amused disbelief, Harmony looks at Rachael and Winnie. Winnie respectfully addresses Rachael and Harmony as she hugs them both goodbye.

"Girls, let me say good night to you and we'll talk later."

They take the hint.

"Good night, Casey," says Harmony.

Ignoring her, Casey taps her foot and disrespectfully looks away.

"Thank you, Winnie," Rachael says as she turns to join Harmony.

They cross the street and walk away together. Relieved to be rid of the intruders, Casey assumes her posture of venting.

"I am trying to explain to you that the Breathalyzer was wrong! Yes, I was speeding and possibly ran a red light. I did make an illegal U-turn. I was driving without a license because I changed purses. And I didn't have my current insurance card and registration in the car, although I am sure they are current. I have no problem admitting all of that and being ticketed. But I was not intoxicated! I had a couple of toasts with champagne at my house that was collectively a glass, or two at the most. You know me! I don't even drink!"

"Casey, I'm sorry this happened to you. I know you must feel terrible but you have to realize the officer was only doing his job. Your Breathalyzer test was—"

"Doing his job? That overzealous, female-phobic, pompous ass! Do you have any idea how humiliating it was for me to be freakin' handcuffed in front of the hotel where I was being honored?"

Empathetically, Winnie looks at Casey and pulls her closer in a one-armed hug. Casey breaks away as she continues to give Winnie her account.

"And Bert! Bert was the gasoline on an already blazing fire. He intentionally insinuated that I was drunk. He deliberately tried to—"

"Casey, Bert was the one who called me. He sounded sincerely concerned."

"Concerned, my ass! I bet he just relished getting to collect my award tonight. He probably had this planned all along, the way he doused me in wine and forced me to have to stay behind and drive myself!"

"Casey, the spillage? Bert planned the spillage? Okay, now you're scarin' me. You know full well that's ridiculous."

Casey contemplates Winnie's comments in silence as she takes out her cellphone and hits speed dial. She reaches Bert's voicemail.

"Yeah, Bert, Casey. I guess you're not in yet from the awards dinner. I, on the other hand, have just been released from jail. You son of a—"

Winnie jerks Casey's arm and stops her from completing her sentence.

"Bert, you are fired! Do you hear me? *Fired!* My attorney will be in touch!"

Chapter 5

Monday morning arrives and Casey is anxious to get back to her good life and put the nightmare of the long, trying weekend behind her. Prohibited from driving until her court date, a limo drops her in front of her building. She walks briskly and makes her way through the revolving doors.

In high gear, she exits the elevator. Annie greets her and hands her the Starbucks triple latte, same as always.

"Casey," Annie whispers sheepishly.

"I know, everyone's waiting for me in the conference room. We definitely have a lot to do."

"Casey, it's not the staff that's waiting."

Casey looks at Annie and simultaneously pushes open the double doors leading into the conference room. Sitting before her and looking much like a firing squad are six members of her Board of Directors, including Ruth Bayslow, Bert Elliott, and Paul Boehlert, attorney for the corporation. Everyone is holding documents and discussing a video of the weekend arrest. Casey's entrance causes everyone to go mute and they stare at her like a deer in headlights.

"What's going on here?" Casey belts out.

"Casey, why don't you have a seat?" suggests Attorney Boehlert.

Casey crosses her arms and continues to stand. Jack enters and plops down a stack of newspapers on the conference table. Like a predator caught, he looks at Casey and quickly darts out of the room without comment.

Paul continues, "Let me first say that all of us feel horrible about this."

Casey places both hands on her hips, shakes her head and fights the urge to explode.

"Casey, please. This is difficult for all of us. Please sit down," Paul implores.

Casey, with fire in her eyes, refuses to comply and remains standing.

"Casey, as senior advisor for Hit Maker Music, I have to inform you that according to your contract as CEO, if you are ever arrested for a crime of moral turpitude, you must step down until the matter is resolved and restitution is made."

"Listen, all of you! There had to be a malfunction with that Breathalyzer. I will do whatever it takes to prove my innocence. I will be exonerated. But in the meantime, I have no intention of relinquishing my position at the company I built!"

A male board member reiterates, "Casey, no one wants this. It's just that it's in the bylaws."

"It's just a formality, Casey. We know you'll be reinstated," offers Ruth, hiding behind her large tote bag that houses the teacup poodle.

"You can't do this to me! I won't have it! You—"

"Casey, I'm sorry but we have no other option." Paul insists emphatically, "We're legally bound. Bert will run the company until after your court appearance. Then we'll decide where things go from there."

"Bert? *No!* Bert is a number cruncher. He's not qualified to run my company!"

Bert replies kindly, "Casey, I'm a businessman. I assure you that I will handle things."

"Bert, you can't handle the simple task of carrying a bottle of wine without spilling it all over innocent bystanders. You alone are to blame for all of this! Had it not been for you none of this would ever have happened! You—"

"Casey, no good can come from being accusatory," says Paul. "According to your contract, Bert is next in line. The rest will have to wait."

Infuriated, Casey turns to exit and smashes open the double doors with both hands. Ruth Bayslow chases her down the hallway and finally succeeds in bringing her to a halt. Ruth holds in her hand Casey's *Woman of the Year* award that she has removed from Casey's office wall. Ruth proceeds with her announcement.

"Casey, I've been instructed by the Guild to retrieve this until the matter is resolved."

"Knock yourself out, Ruth."

Casey goes into her office to gather some of her belongings where she is met by a security guard. He informs her that she is not permitted to remove anything from the premises. Annie runs to Casey's defense.

"Casey, if there is anything you need or anything I can do, please let me know. We'll get through this, Casey."

Casey, in complete shock, musters a look of appreciation.

Jack, Bert, Paul and other Hit Maker Music employees line the hallway and watch as the security guard escorts Casey to the elevator. The ride to the lobby is long and silent. They leave the elevator and walk to the revolving doors where the guard successfully deposits her outside the building.

Carrying nothing but her purse and briefcase, Casey, in a complete daze, stands just outside the entry. She crosses the street and collapses on a park bench. Businessmen and women scurry to and fro as Casey looks up at the Hit Maker Music Building. As hot salty tears well up in her eyes and begin spilling down her face, she looks away and then rummages through her purse for her sunglasses. She stands and begins slowly walking down the sidewalk.

Casey pauses at a newsstand. Her image is on several of the top magazine covers and the front page of *USA Today*. The headline reads, "Record Company Executive, Casey Alliston, Arrested for Numerous Infractions including DUI." As she walks further, she stands beneath a billboard with an image of herself and teenage singing sensation, Erika Marie, holding five platinum records. The caption says, "Hit Maker Music Congratulates Erika Marie Five Million Times." She continues walking.

She crosses another street and enters Piedmont Park. She walks aimlessly as she passes joggers, bikers and parents with strollers. Blankets are spread across the lush green grounds for several yoga enthusiasts engaged in classes. Readers and picnickers relish the clear spring weather. But for the small ripples created by a family of ducks floating by, the duck pond is as smooth as glass. An occasional bass leaps in midair just to make its presence known. From a nearby playground, the sounds of children's laughter and squeaky swing chains permeate the air.

Casey approaches a lemonade stand with a sign overhead that says, *When Life Gives You Lemons, Make Lemonade*. A mime accosts her. She tries ignoring him, but he hands her a red, helium-filled balloon.

Reluctantly she takes it, does an abrupt about face and walks in the opposite direction holding the balloon for only a moment. She releases it and watches it ascend, climbing fast, soaring high and then bursting. *Sort of like my life,* she thinks.

After roaming the park for several hours she calls her limo to take her home. As she drives through the gates of her high rise, reporters are swarming outside of the building. She slumps down in the seat and insists the driver push his way through.

As she walks into her condo, it feels like home. It seems to be more of a refuge than ever before. Her sunroom is furnished with a mixture of art deco and high tech paraphernalia. The easel where she enjoys doing watercolor paintings rests in the corner. A collection of black and white stills of lighthouses and beachscapes line the walls. Casey sits in front of her computer with a cluster of tissue in one hand and a glass of Cabernet in the other, sobbing as she talks to Winnie.

Winnie responds from her tiny, crowded office. She has so many commendations for her community service efforts that they look more like a beautifully painted wall mural than awards. The stack of files on her desk is piled so high she's practically hidden. Soberly, she listens to Casey alternate between explosive venting and heartbreaking devastation. Casey's work is her life and without it, she is void of identity and purpose. Winnie, of all people, understands this. The thought of Casey without her passion scares this longtime best friend.

Exhausted from the events of the last few days, Casey takes a hot bubble bath and slips into her favorite thick terrycloth robe. Surrounded by music industry magazines, she assumes an embryonic position atop her bed. Hot salty tears continue to stream down her face. Never has she felt so betrayed, deserted or out of control.

It would be twelve more days: two hundred eighty-eight more hours or seventeen thousand two hundred eighty minutes until she gets her day in court. How would she ever be able to wait that long to have her future defined? The fear from the *what if's* that cascade through her head is paralyzing. Thankfully, her trance is broken by the sound of the doorbell.

Peering out of the peephole, she sees the only face that has always stuck and always stayed. She opens the door to Winnie holding a Starbucks in one hand and an outstretched arm offering a half hug with the other. Grateful and crying, Casey burrows her head into Winnie's shoulder.

Chapter 6

The courthouse is packed with those awaiting their cases to be called. The room has the typical décor and the strong, stale scent of worn, aged wood. The wood floors creak with every footstep. The presiding Judge Paula Kinard, fiftyish, looks over her bifocals at folders of paperwork. Casey and Winnie stand behind a table in front of the judge and to her right. The prosecutor and Nick are at a table to her left. Winnie has pleaded Casey's case. Officer Patroni has stated his and they await the verdict.

"Ms. Alliston, you plead no contest to all the charges except the DUI?" asks the judge.

"Yes, your honor."

"As Officer Patroni told the court, the Breathalyzer used for your test was completely checked out and there was no malfunction. I will tell you that in many states, the results of your test would be considered substantially under what is considered intoxicated. But unfortunately for you, here in Georgia, you made the mark. We also have eyewitnesses testifying that you had a cocktail party at your home earlier that evening and were seen drinking. Because of those facts, I'm going to let the DUI charges stand. Your sentence will be based on all of the citations."

Winnie puts her arm around Casey's shoulder. Casey glances down, shakes her head in disbelief, and then looks back up at the judge.

"Until this incident, you have been a model citizen and an asset to this community. For that reason, I'm going to be more lenient with you than I normally would be. I'm going to fine you one thousand dollars, send you to driving school and sentence you to serve two hundred community service hours. Your driver's license is suspended for ninety days followed by a year on probation."

Completely incensed, Casey says to Winnie, "*Lenient?*"

Casey decides to jump into the conversation. She figures, what could it hurt?

"Your Honor, may I speak?"

"No, you may not, Ms. Alliston."

Winnie raises her hand and Judge Kinard acknowledges her.

"Yes, Ms. Jenkins?"

"Could we request that Ms. Alliston's community service be served at the Eagle's Nest?"

Astonished and completely stunned with what a terrible suggestion Winnie has proposed, Casey looks at Winnie as though she's lost her mind.

"The Eagle's Nest it is. So ordered."

Judge Kinard strikes her gavel.

"This court is adjourned."

Casey plops down in her chair and puts her head in her hands.

"That was lenient? Seriously? My whole life sucks."

Winnie attempts to console her.

"Casey, it's not the end of the world. You'll be able to put all of this behind you very soon."

Casey continues to talk as though in a trance.

"And you, Wins, even you. Why would you sell me out to a home full of old people and kids?"

"Because I thought you would prefer that to wearing a little orange suit and picking up trash on the highway?"

"Actually I'd prefer the little orange suit, or even Leavenworth. You know I have no use for old people and kids."

As they are gathering their belongings to leave the courtroom, Nick approaches Winnie.

"Seven o'clock work for you?"

"Seven it is. See you then."

Casey stares in disbelief and cannot wrap her mind around what she has just heard. "Winnie! Nick is Dominic? Nick is the new guy you are dating?"

Winnie, expressionless, nods her head in affirmation. Casey picks up her briefcase and leaves abruptly, ignoring Winnie's repeated summons.

"Casey! Casey wait. Casey, please stop!"

As Casey exits the courthouse building, reporters are plentiful. Casey breaks through without comment and is whisked away in her limo. As she arrives at her high rise the media swarm her, shouting, crowding in and assaulting her with questions. As the doorman opens the door, the building manager, Mr. Mason, meets her.

"Ms. Alliston?"

Annoyed, she responds, "Yes, what is it?"

"We've already had several complaints about the media frenzy outside the building. This is the type of attention we frown upon."

He hands her an envelope.

"A formal complaint has been filed. You must adhere to our bylaws or we'll be forced to litigate."

"I have no control over the media!" she fires back in anger. "What do you suggest I do?"

"Give them a statement, Ms. Alliston," he responds sternly.

Casey walks away and presses the elevator button for the penthouse floor. The elevator door opens. Two residents holding different newspapers read and discuss the headlines. They look up, see Casey, become mute and exit as Casey enters. Casey presses the button for her floor and falls back against the wall in frustration.

She enters her condo and heads for her bedroom. She cannot believe how much her life has changed in one day, and it's only 11:30 a.m. She changes into her bathrobe, unplugs the phone and crawls under the covers of her bed. When she awakens the clock reads *2:30 p.m.* She slowly emerges and begins wandering around her house, both hands on her hips. She straightens frames on some of her black and white stills, paints at a half-complete canvas and looks out the window at the street activity below.

After a time, she makes her way into the kitchen. She opens the refrigerator and stares at the abundant collection of unlabeled takeout boxes. She begins tossing them into the trash. From there she goes into the living room, props up on a couple of pillows and thumbs through a few magazines. She wonders how people without jobs survive the boredom. The clock says *6:00 p.m.* For her, this day has lasted a year. A bubble bath, she thinks. *Yes.* That'd be a nice way to end such a long and trying day.

She lights candles, puts on some soothing music and reclines in a full tub of bubbles. After what seems to be the proper length of time for shriveled-up fingers and toes, she lifts herself out and towels off. The clock says *6:35 p.m.* Exasperated, she orders in a veggie pizza.

Casey sits in front of her widescreen television and begins channel surfing. She lands on Home Shopping Network. Casey eats her pie while being completely fascinated by this consumer playground. She has never taken the time to notice this opportunity for great discounts that come without having to deal with traffic or parking. She quickly becomes a fan.

Fully engaged and completely intrigued, the smorgasbord for a shopaholic is irresistible. She orders almost every offering: exercise equipment, Marie Osmond's entire doll collection, a hair removal system, a facial apparatus that replaces having a facelift and an assortment of Chia pets.

She falls asleep on the couch and dreams of how much better life will be once her HSN on-off light clapper arrives so that all she will have to do is clap twice to automatically turn off all her house lights. Because of her love for uniformity, she has ordered a clapper for every light in the condo.

❄ ❄ ❄

As the sun peaks through the east window, Casey jumps up and frantically runs to the shower. She towels off and begins putting on her makeup before waking up enough to realize that she has nowhere to go and nowhere to be.

Wearing sports attire, she exits her building with camera in tow and rides her bike to Piedmont Park. She stops at an outdoor restaurant to have a bagel with coffee and read the paper. She notices several patrons pointing at her and talking. She places her money on the table and leaves her half-eaten breakfast.

She mounts her bike and continues her ride, stopping at various intervals to shoot scenes that capture her attention. Oddly, what seems of interest to her lens is unlike her usual gravitation: a woman feeding pigeons, an old man propped against a tree reading a comic book, a mother and a child examining a huge oak tree, a dog catching a Frisbee and a small child with his dad flying a kite.

She arrives home late afternoon. Her bike basket hosts a bamboo plant and a small bag of groceries. As she enters her kitchen the phone she left behind is on the counter. She checks her phone for voicemails and discovers all three are from Winnie.

"Casey, it's Winnie. Casey? Call me."

Expressionless, Casey hits *delete* and moves to the next message.

"Casey, it's me again. Are you there? C'mon Casey. All right, call me. Will you call me, please? I really want to—"

Before hearing it all, Casey hits delete and listens to the final one.

"Casey, it's—"

She erases the last one without listening.

"Yeah, I know it's you, Winnie."

Casey puts away her groceries and strategically places her bamboo plant on a small table in her sunroom. She makes it through Day Two and wonders how many more she must endure before she gets back her good life.

With shades drawn, her bedroom is pitch black. She sleeps in a big lump under a mound of covers as the phone rings. Twisted and tangled in her cocoon, she's unable to pick up the call before it goes to voicemail. The caller I.D. says it's Winnie.

"Casey, you can't stay mad at me forever."

Casey contemplates her decision and then hits redial. Winnie answers.

"I'm very upset with you, Winifred."

"Casey, met me at Grecco's for lunch?"

After a pregnant pause, Casey responds, "What time?"

"How about 1 p.m.?"

It's a little after 1:30 p.m. as Casey sits in deep concentration, building a configured design out of cocktail straws, coasters, silverware and other available implements from the table. Two empty bottles of Evian are supporting the base. Winnie arrives late.

"Hi Casey. Sorry I'm late."

"No worries. I've discovered a new way to pass time. In fact I'm finding a lot of different ways to pass time."

Winnie immediately confronts the uneasiness.

"Look, Casey, let me say this. I should have told you that Nick was the arresting officer as soon as I knew. But you were so angry, I decided to wait. I was wrong to do that."

Not exactly heartfelt, Casey responds. "I was wrong, too. I apologize."

"Casey, Nick and I are seeing a lot of each other. I really like him and I want you guys to get to know each other."

"Winnie, Nick is to blame for pretty much ruining my life. There's no way in hell I'm going to get to know him. I know enough."

As she glares at Winnie, Casey's restaurant version of Legos topples over and spills across the table. Winnie takes hold of Casey's wrist and addresses her gently, but firmly.

"Casey, Nick was only doing his job. You're always the one talking about how everyone needs to be responsible for their actions. Well, you need to take your own advice. I know this has been a horrible experience for you. But you are to blame for the situation you're in, not Nick, not Bert, and not the public at large."

Reluctantly, Casey listens to the stinging verbal admonishment. Winnie continues.

"Look Casey, why don't you plan on coming with me to church on Sunday. You can stay after and have lunch with us at the Eagle's Nest. I'll introduce you around, that way you can ease your way in."

Contemplating the offer, she replies somewhat sheepishly, "Just the thought of facing Phyllis after I turned her down for a donation …"

"Casey, she's not like that. She'll be glad to see you and glad you're there."

Clueless and in her normal analytical mindset she responds, "Do you think I can count church and lunch toward my hours served? I mean, for me, being there will be reminiscent of a prison sentence."

Winnie looks at her, shakes her head and smiles.

"Let's order lunch, Ms. Cheery."

Following lunch Casey arrives back at her condo where once again the media rushes her. She parks her bike, gets off and finally faces them with a statement.

"I made a mistake. I am paying dearly for it. It is my desire to rectify my error in judgment to the satisfaction of the court and return to making hit records. I have nothing more to say. I will never have more to say. So please respect my privacy and that of the other residents in my building."

Today is a turning point on many levels. Although she is struggling and in pain, Casey is beginning to embrace the fact that sometimes waving the white flag is the best way to leave the past behind and begin anew.

Chapter 7

It was a clear, sunny morning with a slight coolness in the air. The sounds of the choir singing, "God Is Good," meet them halfway down the sidewalk as Casey and Winnie approach the front steps of Christ Community Church.

As they enter the sanctuary, Casey turns into the last pew and plops down like a rock. Immediately mesmerized by Harmony Jones, her former cellmate and the choir director for the church, Casey stares in disbelief as Harmony flaps her arms in overt, broad strokes as if she's attempting to fly.

Winnie gently raises Casey up by the forearm and escorts her further down the aisle to the fourth pew from the podium, then leads her in. Completing the pew is Alex, nine years old, an African-American male dressed like a miniature businessman; Olivia, Asian, seven years old and dressed in a silky blouse, a long skirt and ballet slippers; and Mr. and Mrs. Odrey, late seventies and biracial, who wave and smile at Winnie. The song ends and Harmony steps to the podium. Hoping not to be recognized, Casey slumps down in the pew.

"Good morning, church!"

The congregation responds, "Good morning!"

Harmony continues, "Praise the Lord! It's time to welcome all of our first-time visitors. We just ask that you remain seated so that all of our members can stand and welcome you."

The choir sings, "Everyone is Welcome Here." Casey tries to stand so that she doesn't have to be greeted, but Winnie pushes her back down. Jazzy, a five-year-old, red-headed, freckle-faced little girl wearing a lacy dress, patent leather shoes, a backwards baseball cap and a ball glove on one hand, makes her entrance into the pew. She is itchy from her dress and scratches herself with her glove. She gives Casey the once over.

"You new?"

Casey nods affirmatively as Jazzy extends her left hand. Casey complies and shakes her hand.

"Welcome. You like baseball?"

Winnie answers the question.

"She used to play on an all-girls baseball team at college."

Wide-eyed Jazzy replies, "Cool!"

Jazzy wedges herself in between the end of the pew and Casey, requiring Casey to scoot down just a little. Casey is thrown off guard and Winnie tries to conceal her laughter. Alex, with Olivia in tow, comes down to Casey's end of the pew and shakes Casey's hand.

"Hi, my name is Alex."

"Hi, I'm Casey."

Alex points to Olivia, who is obviously not a blood relative, and says, "This is my sister, Olivia."

Olivia smiles shyly and waves. Casey unenthusiastically waves back.

Alex points to Jazzy, also obviously not a blood relative, and says, "This is my other sister, Jazzy."

Casey casually surveys the multiethnic group and then whispers to Winnie, "Sisters?"

Winnie whispers back. "Don't even try to question it. Alex has been a big brother to many. He takes his role very seriously."

"Alex, Casey and me already met. That's why I'm sittin' here so she don't get lonely. Plus she plays baseball like me."

Grinning proudly, Jazzy looks up at Casey. The Odreys catch Casey's eye, nod and wave. She nods back. Phyllis approaches and Casey squirms.

"Casey, welcome. I'm looking forward to the coming days together. It'll be an honor to have you around. Even if it's just for a season."

Embarrassed, Casey manages to mumble, "Thank you."

Harmony comes over and cheerfully offers a greeting.

"Hello, Casey! Been stayin' out of trouble lately?'

She laughs, as Casey returns a stone-faced look.

"I forgot to ask. You an attorney, too?"

"No, I own a record company."

"A record company?"

Alex lights up. Harmony is enthused and beaming.

"Well, praise the Lord! We need to talk! I'm looking for a record deal for my choir. Did you know that gospel music is the fastest growing music in the world today?"

"So I've heard," mutters Casey in flat monotone.

"Are you staying for lunch?"

Casey nods affirmatively and smiles halfheartedly.

"Good! Can't wait to chat further!"

As the song ends Olivia and Alex wedge their way in between Casey and Winnie and take a seat. Casey squirms a bit at the close proximity. Pastor Joel, a middle-aged man, slight in build and wearing a robe and collar, takes the podium and opens his Bible.

"This morning, I'd like to speak on the life of Job. As most of us know, Job was an extremely wealthy and successful man. To strengthen Job's faith, God allowed him to suffer affliction for a time. Job also lost all of his worldly possessions. But after his testing was over, God restored to him twice what he had lost during his time of difficulty. You see, it is the challenges in life that leave us better off than before."

Casey, bored, checks her watch and counts the dots in the ceiling. Jazzy tries to figure out what Casey is looking at. Winnie taps Casey and gives her a look to pay attention. Pastor Joel continues.

"In this passage, Job says, 'God I know You can do anything and that no thought or purpose of Yours can be stopped. In the past I had only heard of You, but now I have experienced You for myself.' It has always been God's intention that we don't just accept the things we hear about Him but that we experience Him for ourselves."

Pensively, Casey looks at the pastor, then turns away, exhales and checks her watch again. Jazzy looks up at Casey and when she makes eye contact snuggles in closer. Winnie tries not to laugh aloud.

After what seems to be an eternity, church is finally dismissed. Casey, Winnie, Alex, Olivia, Jazzy and the Odreys make their way to the Eagle's Nest dining room. The dining hall is set up with long tables, in family style. Winnie instructs Casey to sit down as she talks with a few of the volunteers. Casey checks her watch. Nick approaches Casey and sits down next to her. She feels like a trapped animal with nowhere to go.

"Casey, I'm over here all the time and I'm sure we're going to run into each other a lot. I was hoping we could put the past behind us and make a fresh start. Truce?"

Nick extends his hand to shake Casey's, who looks guarded but notices Winnie watching.

Without any sincere effort or eye contact she mumbles, "Truce."

The Odreys, Alex, Olivia, Jazzy, Winnie, Harmony, Phyllis, and Nick join Casey at her table. Casey checks her watch. Phyllis stands to greet everyone.

"I hope all of you are enjoying a blessed Lord's Day. Winnie, would you say grace?" They bow their heads and fold their hands, except for Casey who is staring into space. Jazzy sits across from Casey and notices her out of one eye.

"Pssst," Jazzy whispers loudly in a sincere effort to help Casey. "You gotta close your eyes cause we're talkin' to God now."

Casey whispers back as though there is no one else in the room other than Jazzy and her, "Well, I don't actually believe in—"

Winnie gives a look that requires no additional words beyond the mention of her name.

"Casey!"

Casey reluctantly holds her tongue and Winnie prays.

"Dear Lord, thank you for this day, for the food that you have generously provided for us, and for our time together. In Jesus' name, Amen."

Casey, a food snob, is visibly uncomfortable as an overloaded plate of food (unappealing by her standards) is placed in front of her: turkey with all the trimmings. She looks helpless and alternates looking at her plate and looking at Winnie. Winnie gives her a look as Casey reluctantly shovels a small fork full of green beans into her mouth. Jazzy smiles with a mouth full of food as Casey chews and looks at her watch.

"Casey do you have kids?" Alex inquires.

"No," Casey responds emphatically.

Alex, Olivia and Jazzy all smile amongst themselves.

Phyllis interjects, "Casey's going to volunteer with us for a while."

"We're here while our house is being repaired," Mr. Odrey offers.

Somewhat interested, Casey asks, "What happened to it?"

"We practically burned it to the ground," Mrs. Odrey says without emotion.

Casey is wide-eyed and stunned.

"Oh, not on purpose, honey," Mrs. Odrey laughs.

Mr. Odrey continues, "We got distracted in an intense episode of Jeopardy and forgot we were in the middle of making dinner."

"But we answered the grand prize final question correctly," brags Mr. Odrey.

The Odreys laugh lightheartedly. Casey is not sure how to respond.

"Do you have children?"

As though on cue, the Odreys' son, Ken, fortyish, wearing an expensive golf ensemble with his fly open, angrily enters the dining hall carrying some papers. Ken hugs Harmony and kisses her on the cheek. Harmony flirtatiously addresses Ken.

"Hi, Ken. We were hoping to see you at church this morning. Will you be joining us for lunch?"

Obviously irritated, Ken replies, "No, thank you, Harmony. I just stopped in for the same old reason."

Holding up contracts he angrily addresses his parents.

"These are still unsigned. Again!"

Mr. Odrey tactfully tries to get Ken's attention.

"Ah son—"

"Don't interrupt me, Pop. I'm telling you one last time. Give me power of attorney or I will go to court and have you declared incompetent. Then you can stay here permanently!"

Mrs. Odrey gives it another shot.

"But son—"

"Mom, please let me finish. First you burn down your house—"

"Now, son don't exaggerate," Mr. Odrey debates.

Jazzy defends her friends.

"Yeah, Mister Ken, it was only half the house."

Proud to have taken up for them, Jazzy looks at the Odreys and gives them a thumbs up.

Ken continues.

"Then, you wrote a check for five thousand dollars as a gift to the church? After that you gave away your ping pong table to this home.

All in the same week! If you keep up this behavior you'll be left with nothing. Someone has to step in and protect you from yourselves, and that someone is me!"

Winnie steps in.

"Ken, I've decided to take on your parents' case."

"Case? What case?"

"We're filing for a separation," the Odreys state in unison.

"A separation? You've been married for almost fifty years!"

"Not from each other, son. From you," says Mr. Odrey.

"From me? But I'm your son!"

"Yes you are! And we love ya," proclaims Mrs. Odrey.

"You're too big and too old for us to send you to your room," adds Mr. Odrey.

The kids cover their mouths and laugh.

"So we're doing what we feel is necessary until you start behaving in a more acceptable manner," declares Mrs. Odrey.

"What? Look, there can be no argument that they need constant supervision!"

Winnie continues. "In my opinion there's nothing incompetent about your parents. How they spend their money is really up to them. And in regard to the stove, everyone forgets things on occasion. It happens to the best of us."

"But, they forget even the smallest things, Winnie! That is dangerous!"

"Like I said, it happens even to the best of us. For instance, apparently you forgot to zip your fly. That's a simple thing. Does that mean we need to ready a room for you?"

"That was a good one," Jazzy states with enthusiastic approval.

Ken looks down, turns to zip up and heads toward the door in a huff. The Odreys look resigned.

"Son, aren't you forgetting something?" asks Mr. Odrey.

Mrs. Odrey chimes in, "What if today was our last day on earth?"

Frustrated, Ken turns and comes back to hug his parents.

"You're both making me crazy!"

"Oh, Ken, you don't mean that," Mrs. Odrey says lovingly.

Ken leaves the paperwork and turns to leave.

"Mom and Dad, please sign these. I'm trying to do what's best. I'll call you later, Harmony."

Harmony places her hands over her heart and then fans herself.

"He's testy, but he's so fine!"

Harmony watches Ken exit and then turns to Casey.

"So Casey, tell me about your record label?"

All eyes are on Casey as she sighs and looks at her watch.

"There's really nothing to tell. We put out a lot of music but have no plans for expanding to include the gospel market. I'm just not interested in your genre."

"Well, my Bible tells me that God can turn the hearts of kings like a rudder on a ship," Harmony says with conviction. "So I will just make it a matter of prayer that if it's God's will He will change your mind," Harmony smiles confidently.

Slightly irritated, Casey responds, "You can pray all you want, but I can tell you with all certainty that you're wasting your time."

Casey looks at her watch again, stands, tells everyone goodbye and heads for the exit.

"I'll call you later," says Winnie.

"Sounds good."

Casey walks home alone pondering all the events of this Sunday. Church, a sermon, gospel music, orphans, old people, praying before meals, strange foods and conversation about many things completely foreign to her world. All she can think about is how she will possibly be able to endure one hundred ninety-seven more hours.

Chapter 8

The Driver's School is tucked away down a heavily traveled side street on the east side, located in an old brick building with burglar bars. Casey, in sweats, examines the piece of paper in her hand where she has scribbled the address and confirms she is at the right place.

She enters the building and takes a rickety elevator to the third floor. She can hear the rumble of muted conversation coming from a room down the hall.

As she walks into the room, attendees are socializing like it's ole home week, introducing themselves and some are even exchanging phone numbers. A young woman in her early twenties wearing a sweatsuit two sizes too small spots a bleached-blonde male bodybuilder across the room. She enthusiastically bounces over to him. They embrace and Casey listens in on the exchange as she checks her phone messages.

"Hans, what are you doing here?"

"Too much vodka in my fruit smoothies," he replies in a heavy Swedish accent.

"Shame on you! Are you doing the four, six or eight o' clock class today?"

Hans strikes a bodybuilder pose and says, "All three!"

They laugh, as Casey, bewildered, lifts her brow.

A middle aged woman with thick makeup and big hair applies the fifth layer of bright orange lipstick as a slender guy with a Hispanic accent wearing a halter top and biker pants approaches her.

"Excuse me lovely lady, but I must know the flavor of that fabulous color lipstick?"

Flattered she proudly responds, "It's Passion Mango, handsome."

To Casey's left a young twenties couple exchange phone numbers.

The young man exclaims, "I have never felt such gravitation toward someone I've just met. This is so strong!"

The female responds excitedly, "I feel the same way. Maybe at lunch we could go to my place!"

Casey closes her eyes and shakes her head just as the Driver's School instructor enters the room. He is short, round and bald. He wears glasses and a large whistle around his neck. He blows the whistle to silence the room.

"Listen up people. We have a lot to cover today. First we're going to watch a film that covers all the basics of good defensive driving. Then we're going to choose partners and go to the hospital down the street to view cadavers that died because of speeding, drunk driving, or road rage."

He dims the lights and the film begins.

"When you first enter the vehicle, adjust your mirrors and your seat. Fasten your seatbelt. This is the steering wheel."

Casey hears moaning sounds and glances a couple desks away to see the young twenties couple making out. The film lasts about twenty minutes and covers all the basics of driving. The instructor turns the lights back up.

"Okay, choose a partner for our field trip to view the cadavers."

Casey stands and turns around. Harmony Jones waves both arms at her from the rear of the room.

"Casey, Casey! I got here just after the film started and didn't spot you until now. I can't believe God has blessed me to be the buddy of a record company president! I got busted for speeding in the church bus. What'd they get you for?"

"Speeding in the church bus? Dang, girl, you sure get arrested a lot!"

"Yeah, well …"

Enroute to the hospital, the class walks down the sidewalk as Harmony talks Casey's ear off. She continues talking even as they view the cadavers. Casey has a horrendous case of verbiage overload. All she wants is for Harmony to shut up. She decides that she will escape to a restroom for an ear break. However, Harmony follows her.

Casey sits inside a stall where she now hears Harmony's voice slightly amplified and echoed.

Harmony says, "I'm all done, buddy! I'll wait for you outside."

"Yeah, good. Do that. I'll be out in a minute. A long minute," she mumbles.

"Oh, I got ya, girl. You just probably have the runs because you're upset about those cadavers. You take your time and I'll go find you a soda. Something fizzy should calm you down."

"No, that's okay. Really. I'll be fine. Just give me a minute."

"Oh, girl, no need to thank me. I'm happy to help. The heartbreak of diarrhea is nothing to be ashamed of. Ain't no one on the planet who's lived life without having an unwanted case of the squirts. I'll be back in a jiff."

"But I don't have diarrhea!"

"You're in denial. I understand. But I'm still gonna help you."

Completely frustrated, Casey replies, "Okay, whatever!"

Harmony exits the bathroom leaving Casey alone in her stall. Like a newly crowned queen, she sits atop the toilet seat and makes a call to Winnie.

"Dang, Winnie, Harmony talks incessantly. Wouldn't you think the sight of a corpse would have warranted at least a slight pause? She doesn't even breathe between paragraphs!"

"Harmony's just friendly, Casey. Take a few deep breaths and keep it in perspective. It's only for half a day."

"Half a day? She'll be within spitting distance of me for every second of my 200 hours of community service at the Eagle's Nest! Have you gotten any word on my reinstatement?"

"Not yet. Be patient."

Just then the bathroom door swings open and Harmony walks in holding a cup with ice and club soda.

"Casey? Casey, buddy? You still in here? I got you something cold and fizzy. I promise it will help."

Harmony bangs on the outside of Casey's stall.

"Casey, can you hear me?"

Harmony stoops down and looks under the stall door. Casey, still on the phone with Winnie, throws her head back and sighs.

"I gotta go," she says as she ends the call with Winnie.

"I know you gotta go," says Harmony as she locks eyes with her from beneath the stall. "That's what diarrhea is. You gotta go!"

Harmony passes off the cup of soda to Casey under the stall door. Casey leans forward and takes it.

"Thank you," Casey says quietly.

"Oh, you're welcome, buddy. Believe me, I've been there!"

Casey concedes and sips on her soda while still isolated behind the stall door, the only thing temporarily protecting her from the inevitable.

Chapter 9

A limo pulls up to the curb outside the Eagle's Nest. Casey and Harmony exit with Harmony still chattering. As they enter the home, the children are being organized into small groups for their field trip to Barnes and Noble with their assigned chaperones.

"Hello my little precious ones," Harmony sings.

Hearing Harmony's voice, Alex, Olivia and Jazzy turn toward her. But their sights are on Casey. They run to greet her, giving her a group hug.

"Casey!" they exclaim enthusiastically.

Casey, happy to be rescued from Harmony's incessant chatter, returns their welcome with a guarded amount of warmth. As though concerned about their inoculation status, she reservedly pats them about the back and shoulders. Phyllis enters the room and greets everyone.

"Good afternoon, everyone. Thanks for coming. We've divided the children into groups of two or three to maximize one-on-one time at the bookstore. Casey: Alex, Olivia and Jazzy have requested you as their special friend today."

Casey looks uneasy with the thought that anyone under thirty and not in her business world would request her for anything.

She responds, "And how long will we be there?"

"Usually a couple of hours."

Casey sets her watch.

With that, everyone files outside and makes their way onto the church bus. Mr. Odrey drives and Mrs. Odrey sits in the seat just behind him. Casey makes her way to the last seat in the back as Alex, Olivia and Jazzy, wearing her baseball glove, follow behind her like little puppies. Once she sits down, they all try to squeeze into the same seat to be close to her.

"There's plenty of room, you know. We don't have to be squashed into one seat."

Alex motions Olivia to come with him to the seat across the aisle. Jazzy looks up at Casey and scoots closer to her. Casey exhales and looks at her watch.

When they arrive at Barnes and Noble, the first thing Casey does is drag the children to the café. She buys a vente latte, a *New York Times* and snacks for the kids. Then she corrals them to sit down at a big round table. She passes out the snacks, opens her paper and begins to drink her coffee and read.

After about ten minutes, she lowers her paper to find all three children staring at her.

"Okay kids, here's the deal. Alex, take your sisters upstairs and all of you pick out a book. Then if all three of you will sit at the table and be very quiet reading your books, I'll buy your books for you to keep! How's that sound?"

The expression on the faces of the kids is one of grave disappointment. Casey, still not connecting the dots, tries to negotiate.

"What?"

They continue to stare at her.

"Okay, you can each pick two books."

Compliantly, Alex helps the girls up from the table, brushes off their hands and mouths, and escorts them to the escalator. Casey goes back to reading her newspaper as Mr. and Mrs. Odrey approach the table.

"Casey are we going to be seeing you tomorrow?" asks Mrs. Odrey.

"You'll be seeing me most everyday for a while."

Mr. Odrey chimes in.

"Do you think you could take us for our doctors' appointments tomorrow? We have to have someone with us to drive us home."

Casey gazes over the top of her paper and checks her watch. She listens without expression.

"It's our annual colonoscopy," explains Mrs. Odrey. "It's at ten o'clock. Our son was supposed to take us but …"

Rolling her eyes, "Yeah, I know, but you're separated. I guess, sure okay."

Mrs. Odrey pats both sides of Casey's face. Mr. Odrey smiles at her and pats her on the back. They go back to their table. She stares at them and resumes reading her paper.

Upstairs in the children's department, Alex, Olivia and Jazzy stand before a large display of the popular children's book and sing-along song, *Wonder What Will Davey Bring Home Next?* Alex encourages his sisters.

"Casey is new and doesn't have the hang of things yet. She just needs some time to get to know us. That's all. I'm sure she'll learn to like us."

Olivia nods affirmatively.

"Course she likes us," argues Jazzy. "She's buyin' us books ain't she? And she already got us good snacks."

Alex takes the books he has chosen for himself along with two copies of *Wonder What Will Davey Bring Home Next?* for Olivia and Jazzy and escorts the girls back downstairs to Casey's table where they find her perusing a *Billboard Magazine* and still drinking her coffee. Alex places all the books on the table. Alex and Olivia take a seat as Jazzy summons her.

"Casey?"

There is no response. Slightly amused, the Odreys observe the attempt at interaction.

"Casey?"

Still no response. With that, Jazzy climbs up on a chair and shouts at the top of her lungs.

"Casey!"

Startled, Casey lowers her magazine and checks her watch.

"Jazzy you shouldn't yell like that. What is it? And sit down, will you?"

Jazzy complies.

"Will you read my books to me?"

"Can't Alex or Olivia read them to you?"

"Olivia don't talk."

"Why doesn't Olivia talk?"

"She's sittin' right here, why don't you ask her yourself?"

"Well if I ask her, how will she answer me if she doesn't talk?"

Jazzy shrugs her shoulders as Olivia shyly looks at the floor. Alex, slightly perturbed, weighs in.

"Olivia'll talk when she's ready. She just doesn't have anything to say."

Alex continued, "Look Casey, they're used to our volunteers reading to them. That's the whole idea you know—interaction."

Casey rolls her eyes, puts down the newspaper, guzzles her last bit of coffee and grabs a book. Sitting across the table from the girls, Casey begins to read *Wonder What Will Davey Bring Home Next?* She reads fast, monotone and with no feeling or differential in the voices of the characters.

My name is Lily and I am nine years old. My little brother Davey is six and likes to bring home lost, homeless or hurt animals. Our Mom and Dad told him he can help any animal he finds but we can't adopt any more or we will need a bigger house.

One night, I was walking down the hallway toward my room when I heard my little brother Davey's door open ever so slightly. I turned to see what was going on.

"Pssst," Davey whispered to get my attention.

When I turned to look, all I could see was one eye peaking at me and Davey's index finger motioning me to come in. And so, I did.

"What is it?" I asked.

"Shhhhhh," Davey replied and then shut the door behind us.

Then, he sang me this song he made up.

> *There's an owl in my closet*
> *Don't you dare tell Mom and Dad*
> *There's an owl in my closet.*
> *Best owl I ever had*
> *Gonna keep him till he's better, oh yeah*
> *Cause he's my owl.*

Jazzy interrupts. "Casey I can't see the pictures. And Casey, you gotta read slower so we can pretend we don't know what's going to happen and it will be like a surprise. And you gotta make Lily and Davey's voices sound different from each other. Like this!" she says with great excitement. In a deep voice and with facial expressions she demonstrates from memory.

"What is it?" I asked.

"Shhhhhh," Davey replied and then shut the door behind us.

Then, he sang me this song he made up.

Jazzy sings the song perfectly.

> *There's an owl in my closet*
> *Don't you dare tell Mom and Dad*
> *There's an owl in my closet.*

> *Best owl I ever had*
> *Gonna keep him till he's better, oh yeah*
> *Cause he's my owl.*

"You mean you've already heard this story?"

"Yes, but we like it. That's why we want to hear it again. See, if you don't read it like that it's just won't be as joyable."

Olivia nods affirmatively and Casey sighs. Alex takes the opportunity to correct Jazzy.

"*Enjoyable*, Jazzy, not *joyable*."

Jazzy mumbles the word *enjoyable*.

"Casey do you mind if we move to one of the couches?" Alex suggests. Casey surrenders and complies.

The girls cuddle up to Casey and they look like a family portrait. Alex sits on the floor reading his own book. Casey resumes reading with inflection and character distinction in her voice. In a very high-pitched voice Casey continues.

> *Then, Davey led me over to his closet. He opened the door and reached way in the back. He pulled out a shoebox that had holes in the top of it. He opened it.*
>
> *I could not believe my eyes! Much to my surprise, there lying on top of several nice soft socks was a little baby owl.*

Jazzy lifts Casey's arm and snuggles up. Olivia closes in as well. Alex looks up at them and smiles broadly. Casey looks awkward, checks her watch and continues in a whiny tone.

> *I said good night to Davey and his new friend and headed to my own bedroom. I crawled into my nice warm bed and started thinking about Davey. What if he started finding larger or even wild animals roaming about our neighborhood? A buffalo … an elephant … a parrot … a monkey? Only time will tell. I wonder what will Davey will bring home next?*

Just as Casey finished the book, the Odreys signaled it was time to leave. As promised, Casey paid for the books. She was happy to have logged the hours and glad the only thing remaining was the ride home.

As the bus pulls up to the Eagle's Nest, fire trucks are pulling away. Everyone exits the bus as Phyllis, along with Nick, Winnie and Harmony approach. Backpacks and duffle bags line the curb.

"What happened?" asks Casey.

"We had a fire break out in one of our storage areas," said Phyllis.

Nick continues, "They haven't determined the cause, so until they check out all of our wiring and determine that everything is in order, they want us evacuated."

"How long do they think it will take?" inquires Mr. Odrey.

"Shouldn't be more than twenty-four hours," says Winnie.

"We just need to get everyone situated for the night," replies Harmony.

"Casey you could knock out a lot of hours with a spend-the-night party," teases Winnie.

Casey looks horrified.

Mr. Odrey jumps in, "That'll work out perfectly! Casey is taking us to our doctors' appointments tomorrow. This way, we'll already be with you and you won't even have to come and pick us up!"

"Okay, I'll take the Odreys," replies Casey as she turns toward her limo.

Winnie smiles broadly and continues.

"And Harmony can come by first thing in the morning and get the kids."

"Kids?"

With that, the kids excitedly grab their backpacks and hurl themselves in the back of Casey's limo. The Odreys follow the kids. Casey examines the cargo in her backseat, shakes her head, gives Winnie a look and opens a passenger door to sit in the front seat.

The sunset is particularly stunning with blended hues of orange, peach and purple. Casey stares out the passenger-side, front-seat window of the vehicle. She drinks in a quiet moment of peace in anticipation of heaven only knows what the rest of the evening will entail.

In the rear cabin, Alex, Olivia and Jazzy watch TV and play with the phone. Jazzy presses the button to lower the window separating the front and back seats. Casey turns, looking slightly miffed. Jazzy smiles and waves as Alex puts it back up.

The limo makes its final turn into the main entranceway of Casey's Midtown high rise. The children and the Odreys are wide-eyed as the limo passes through the security gate and stops at the entrance where a uniformed doorman greets them.

As they exit the limo, the doorman and Casey exchange greetings. Everyone follows Casey into the lobby and onto the elevator. They ride to the top floor and exit, walking down a long, wide hallway to number 2308. Casey opens the door to a spacious, luxurious and elegant living space. Black and white photos of nautical scenes line the walls. There is a side table with three framed pictures of lighthouses. Jazzy, Alex and Olivia examine the photos.

"Casey, how come you don't have no pictures of people?" Jazzy inquires.

"What do you mean?"

"You just have pictures of boats and giant candles, not no people."

"Giant candles?"

Casey looks at the frames.

"Those are lighthouses, Jazzy. They help guide ships, so they can see at night and in stormy weather."

With her hands on her hips and with all due manner of seriousness Jazzy replies, "Casey that's just what I said! They're giant candles!"

Casey rolls her eyes as Jazzy continues.

"But where's your people?"

The Odreys listen for an answer but Casey ignores the question. Instead, she summons Alex to follow her down the hall to his designated digs for the night. The décor is a nautical theme in navy, white and lime green. The king-size bed has a soft, thick comforter stacked with various sized pillows. There's a footstool on the right side for the vertically challenged.

"It's all yours," declares Casey.

"Thanks, Casey."

Next, Casey shows the Odreys their bedroom. The décor is elegant and formal. Mr. Odrey tests the four-poster bed.

"Thanks for putting us up, Casey."

"No problem."

"This is just lovely," adds Mrs. Odrey. "I'll be right out to help you with the girls."

Casey returns to the living room to find the girls missing.

"Hey girls, where are you?"

"Out here!"

Casey follows the voices to her sunroom where she finds Jazzy and Olivia standing before her treasured easel and art supplies, each one busily painting an original.

"Hey, you guys! Those are my paints and you have no right to touch them!"

Startled, Jazzy and Olivia put down the paintbrushes. Jazzy boldly motions for Casey to bend down to her level. Casey complies.

"Casey, you gotta learn how to share. Harmony says selfish ain't nice."

"*Isn't* nice," Casey fires back.

"What?"

"Selfishness, *isn't* nice."

"That's what I said, Casey! It sure ain't, so why were you mad we were sharin' your paints?"

Casey, slightly taken aback, ignores the question just as Mrs. Odrey appears on the scene.

"Girls are you ready for Casey to show you where you will sleep?"

Meekly they nod their heads.

"Casey will lead the way."

With that, Casey shows them to a generously sized room with twin beds and decorated in earth tones. Original paintings of oceanscapes, seagulls, tortoises and glass containers full of shells warmly frame the space. Mrs. Odrey helps them unpack their pajamas. She gives the girls a look and Jazzy responds.

"Thank you, Casey."

Olivia quietly approaches Casey and hugs her around her legs.

"You're welcome. Sleep well."

And with that, Casey retreats to her bedroom for her long, hot, relaxing nightly bubble bath.

After a long soak, wearing an oversized terrycloth bathrobe, she turns down the covers and plops into her king-size bed. She picks up the *Coastal Living* magazine on her nightstand and begins perusing it. Reaching for her water bottle, she realizes it's empty. She climbs back out of bed and heads for the kitchen.

As she opens her bedroom door, she hears the song, "In the Wee Small Hours of the Morning," coming from the Odreys' bedroom. She slows her pace as she passes the doorway. The Odreys are slow dancing.

They talk tenderly to one another. Casey is moved and about to resume her quest for water, when the Odreys notice her. They slide across the room and embrace her in a three-way dance.

"Now you should be forewarned that if you continue making us feel so wanted and welcome, we may just have to adopt you," says Mr. Odrey.

"Always did want a daughter," Mrs. Odrey chimes in.

Uncomfortable, Casey politely breaks the encirclement. Before resuming their dance, they pull her back in, hug her goodnight, kiss her cheeks and thank her for the hospitality. Pensively, Casey walks away but turns to catch one last glimpse before exiting. They smile and blow kisses.

Casey wanders back through the living room. Her framed pictures on the sideboard catch her eye. Thinking about Jazzy's earlier observation, she thoughtfully picks up a few of her framed pictures, looks them over and then methodically sets them back down.

Suddenly, she's no longer tired. She opens the French doors leading out onto her expansive balcony. Then, as she so often does when her nights get restless, she makes herself a latte, lights up a cigar and sits down in her favorite spot overlooking the city. The view is spectacular. Finally, some peace. At last, some solitude.

Without warning, Casey is startled when Jazzy, wearing her pajamas and carrying her Teddy bear, walks out onto the balcony. She gives Casey one look and bursts into tears.

"What's wrong? Did you have a bad dream?"

Casey gets no response, just intensified bellowing.

"Wait here, I'll get Mrs. Odrey."

Casey puts down her coffee mug and cigar and stands. Jazzy grabs her around the legs and continues sobbing.

"You're gonna die," declares Jazzy.

"I'm gonna die? What are you talking about?"

"I learned it at Kindergarten."

"What? What did you learn?"

"Smoking'll kill ya!"

Mumbling and rolling her eyes Casey says to herself, "Oh my gosh."

Casey bends down to Jazzy's level and looks her in the eye.

"Jazzy, I don't really smoke."

Jazzy continues to whimper.

"That's a cigar. I don't even inhale."

"What's inhale?"

Frustrated and too tired to deal with it, Casey attempts to smooth it over.

"Oh never mind. Don't worry, it's not important. Did you need something?"

Jazzy is still upset but beginning to calm down. In a quivery voice she continues her plea.

"Promise you'll never smoke again?"

"I don't know if I …"

Jazzy starts tearing up.

"Okay, okay, I promise."

Jazzy throws her arms around Casey's neck, then she holds Casey's face in her hands.

"Can you bring me to my room and tuck me in, Casey?"

"Maybe we should get Mrs. Odrey."

Jazzy takes her by the hand and leads her back inside the house.

"It's not hard. I can show ya."

After tucking in Jazzy and making sure Olivia has all the covers she needs, Casey looks in on Alex who plays video games and looks like the king of his castle.

"Alex, lights out. You have school tomorrow."

"Okay, Casey."

As she slips back into bed, she affixes her blinders over her eyes and burrows down under the covers for a good night's rest. She is glad these house guests are only here for one night and that at least for the inconvenience she is racking up community service hours. The pay-off in the mix helps her doze off with some semblance of satisfaction.

Chapter 10

As the alarm sounds, the clock says 7:00 a.m. Casey sits up in bed with her eye mask in place. There is a knock at the door. Outside her bedroom, the kids and the Odreys are dressed and holding a breakfast tray of eggs, bacon, toast, pancakes with fruit, juice and coffee. Startled and still foggy Casey responds.

"Yes?"

As her bedroom door opens, Casey raises the eye mask to rest atop her head and squints as everyone cheerfully enters her room. Horrified, Casey modestly pulls the covers up to her neck and tries to focus. Mrs. Odrey places the tray across her lap. Everyone cheerfully sings "Good Morning to You!" Casey stares in disbelief. Mr. Odrey lifts the blinds, causing Casey to squint. She pulls her mask back down halfway over her eyes. Mr. Odrey launches into an account of the morning activities thus far.

"Good morning, sunshine! We went to the market early this morning."

"Yeah, you didn't have no food in your frigerator," Jazzy chimes in.

"Any food, Jazzy. I didn't have any food in my refrigerator."

Jazzy looks at the others and shrugs. She whispers to Olivia, "Ain't that zactly what I said?"

Olivia nods affirmatively.

"Maybe she can't hear good?"

Olivia nods.

"The kids wanted to make you a special breakfast," says Mrs. Odrey.

Casey squints and stares at the food.

"Thank you," Casey says, still half asleep.

"Taste it!" Alex suggests enthusiastically.

Momentarily sparing her, Casey's phone rings, delaying the battle over too much early morning activity. She answers.

"Yes? Okay, send her on up." She ends the call, adding sarcastically, "And anyone else who might be wandering around the neighborhood."

"That was the doorman. Harmony's on her way up to get the kids."

Alex, Olivia and Jazzy jump up onto the bed with Casey and begin thanking her for letting them stay over. The doorbell rings and Mrs. Odrey exits to answer it. She returns with Harmony, who's also wide awake and cheery. She plops down on Casey's bed.

"Good morning, Casey!"

"Hello."

"What a wonderful looking breakfast!"

"We made it for her," Alex says proudly.

"You want some breakfast too, Harmony? Scoot up there by Casey and share some of hers," Jazzy suggests.

Freaked out at the thought, Casey addresses the Odreys.

"Ah, I really need to get a shower so we're not late for your appointment."

The Odreys comply.

"Come along, children. Let's get your things together for school."

With that, Casey holds onto her tray as the kids bounce toward her to give her hugs and then exit. Harmony heads for the door, as well.

"Have a day that is highly blessed and favored of the Lord!"

Casey squints and waves as Harmony closes the door behind her.

Completely disconcerted by the morning activity, Casey puts down her tray and dials Winnie.

"Winnie Jenkins, how may I help you?"

"Wins it's me. Oh my gosh! Can you please try and get me reinstated today! I'm begging you!"

"Casey, you sound unduly alarmed."

"Listen, when I awakened this morning I had five people standing over me with ah, ah, a buffet of breakfast food."

In an effort not to expose her laughter, Winnie covers the phone. Casey continues.

"Then, Harmony arrives and plops down on my bed with the rest of them!"

Winnie laughs even more.

"It was like, like... camp! Okay, I know I never actually went to camp. But had I gone, I believe this is what it would have been like. Wins, I'm going nuts here. I have to go back to work. Preferably today, okay?"

Winnie tries to compose herself.

"Casey, I'm sorry you had such an action-packed morning. But, I'm fairly certain the Board of Directors is going to have you serve at least half of your hours before they will consider reinstating you."

"Half the hours? C'mon!"

"Be patient. I'm working on it."

Disappointed she replies, "Okay. Thanks, Wins."

Casey ends the call, stands, picks up a piece of toast, takes and bite and heads for the shower.

The Odreys sit in the living room awaiting Casey to take them to their medical appointment. Finally, her bedroom door opens and she appears, dressed in casual attire, carrying her briefcase and camera and talking on her cell phone. She motions the Odreys to follow her out the door.

They take the long elevator ride to the lobby where outside the limo awaits.

The driver opens the door for them as Casey continues her phone conversation.

"Look! This is the third time I have called this morning. You tell Annie to call me at once!"

She ends the call.

The driver inquires, "What hospital are we going to?"

"Northside," they all reply in unison.

Casey opens her briefcase and begins reviewing papers. Mrs. Odrey holds Mr. Odrey's hand and pats him with the other. Mr. Odrey kisses her hand. Casey watches their interaction and then goes back to reading.

Upon arriving at the hospital, the Odreys get checked in and are wheeled down the hall for their procedures. Casey sits in the waiting area reviewing business documents. Her cell phone rings.

"Hello? Annie? What's up with you? I've left you a number of messages! What took you so long to return my calls?"

"I haven't gotten any messages. I was just calling to see how you're doing."

What neither Casey nor Annie realize is that in an effort to cut off all communication and create dissension amongst the troops, Jack has been discarding any messages that Casey has left for Annie.

Dr. Virginia Critelli approaches, interrupting their conversation.

"Excuse me? Are you Casey Alliston?"

Casey looks confused, but affirms, "Yes."

"The Odreys described you to me."

"I see."

Casey addresses Annie.

"Annie I have to go. I'll call you later."

As the call ends Dr. Critelli points to a sign on the wall that says, *Please refrain from using any cellular or electronic equipment.*

"Sorry."

Dr. Critelli shares her findings.

"Mr. Odrey's heart condition is about the same. Just try to keep him exercising and on the low-fat, high-fiber diet. I'm afraid the prognosis for Mrs. Odrey isn't as good. I found a couple of new polyps. Since the first ones we removed were cancerous, I expect these may be, too. But we'll have to wait for the biopsy to come back. "

Casey, seeming concerned, responds, "Is she going to be okay?"

"You know Mrs. O. She's a trooper. Remember, originally we only gave her a few months. She's already beaten all the odds."

Surprisingly disturbed Casey says, "A few months? Do they know everything you're telling me? I mean … they seem so happy."

"Oh yes, they know everything. They just don't let their circumstances define their happiness. And they certainly give credence to the benefits of having a positive attitude and making every second count."

Becoming irritated Casey asks, "Does their son know about this?"

Two nurses appear, pushing the Odreys who have their hands clasped together and ride side by side in wheelchairs. Mrs. Odrey addresses Casey.

"You ready dear? Life awaits!"

"Wanna race?" Mr. Odrey teases.

"I guess you'd better go," says the Dr. Critelli, smiling.

Contemplatively, Casey watches their uncompromising joy as they're wheeled past her toward the limo outside.

MAKE LEMONADE

This morning, Hit Maker Music feels more like a morgue than a record company. One of their star clients, Erika Marie and Bud, her manager and father, are expected for what Bud has termed a life-or-death, make-it-or-break-it meeting with all the honchos, except for Casey (of course) who is prohibited from attending.

As the elevator door opens and they both exit, Annie greets them in the reception area.

"Well hello, Erika and Mr. Marie."

"Now that Casey's out of the picture, I need to see whoever's in charge," he states matter-of-factly.

"Oh, Casey's not out of the picture, Mr. Marie. In fact I just—"

"I'm not interested in your spin. Who's taken over?" he replies abruptly.

"Yes, sir. If you'll please follow me."

Annie leads the two down a long, wide hallway into Bert's office. The office is spacious, with a large rosewood desk and rich, deep gold, green and rose-colored furnishings. A wall of windows overlook the Atlanta skyline. Bert stands to greet them but even before he is able to complete his greeting, Bud blasts him with the bottom line.

"I'll get right to the point. We want out of our recording contract with Hit Maker Music. All this bad press affiliated with drunk driving and disrespecting the law is not good for Erika's image. Her option for renewal comes up in a month. We're not renewing."

"Please, Mr. Marie have a seat," Bert requests.

Bud, Erika Marie and Annie, with her laptop in hand to take notes, all take their seats.

"Bud, we've got a lot invested here. Casey made Erika a household name. And we have two more options on her contract."

"Erika's talent made her a household name. And we've made you tons of money. The relationship was mutually beneficial, but now the honeymoon's over. Our contract has a clause for issues of moral turpitude. I've already checked with my attorney. The charges against Casey fall under that description. Casey's a *convict!*"

Down the hall and inside the closed door to his office, Jack has his intercom on to eavesdrop on the conversation. Smugly, he picks up the phone to make a call. Bert continues trying to manage the situation.

"You are planning to complete the tour, aren't you?"

Bud's anger intensifies.

"Two sponsor reps came to the concert last night. They said they have gotten tons of hate mail from patrons criticizing their involvement with a company whose CEO has been arrested, and for drunk driving! The tour is all but cancelled!"

Annie joins in the effort. "Mr. Marie, please don't make a decision without first speaking with Casey. She's been so hands-on with Erika's career. Let us try to arrange a conference call."

Mr. Marie stands and hands Bert termination papers.

"Are you people deaf or just stupid? It's over! We're done here! How many ways do I need to say it?"

"But Daddy! Can't we talk to Casey first? I really think …"

"You're not in this, Missy!"

Erika begins to tear up.

"But, I love Casey, she—"

"Erika enough! Just be quiet. I'm handling this!"

"I'll escort you to the elevator," offers Annie.

"No need."

Bud takes Erika by the arm and leads her out of the offices to the lobby elevator. Jack enters the elevator uninvited.

"I have something that may be of interest to you, Mr. Marie."

The elevator door closes.

Annie exits Bert's office and immediately calls Casey. "Casey, it's Annie. You need to call me as soon as you get this."

Chapter 11

It's late afternoon as Winnie sits at her desk across from Ken, who is holding an armful of paperwork and looking unusually somber.

"Ken, your parents aren't incompetent. They are capable of living where ever they choose."

"I have a letter from a certified psychiatrist saying otherwise."

"Ken, the shrink is your golf partner. I think the court would view that as a conflict of interest. What is the real issue here?"

"Winnie, if they run out of money I'm not prepared to deal with it. I'm afraid if I don't have power of attorney they're going to give away every dime they have to the church or the home."

"Would that be such a bad thing? I mean, it is their money."

"But they are so old and fragile."

"Old and fragile? Your parents are so much fun! They're full of life!"

"Yeah, that's what Harmony says."

"Take some time and get to know them, Ken, adult to adult. I think it'll put your mind at ease. Really."

Ken nods indicating agreement. Unannounced, Casey barges through the door.

"Oh, I'm sorry, I didn't know you were with a client."

Ken turns around and Casey recognizes him.

"You're the Odreys' son, right?"

"Yeah."

Controlled, but slowly mounting her high horse, Casey throws out some unsolicited advice.

"Listen, I don't generally get into other people's affairs but your parents are good people. You need to spend more time with them. I took them to their doctors' appointments today and, well, you just need to."

Ken stands and faces Casey.

"I know. Thanks for taking them, Casey."

Taken aback, Casey replies, "No problem."

"I'm headed to make amends now."

Ken exits and Winnie can't resist the opportunity to tease Casey.

"Well, that sounded very crusader-ish!"

Casey rolls her eyes and ignores her.

"Right. Listen, can you come with me to my offices later? I need to pick up a few things so I can do some work at home."

"Sure, happy to escort you."

Ken stops by a local florist, buys a beautiful bouquet of flowers and heads to Christ Community Church. As he walks into the church, a children's choir is being dismissed on the main floor. He sits on a back pew. Harmony hugs several of the children as they exit. She steps to the podium and readjusts her music on the music stand as the full adult choir files in for rehearsal. The Odreys enjoy sitting on the front row listening to all the beautiful music.

"Now remember, I'm trying to get us a record deal, so I want you to sing it like you mean it," Harmony exhorts.

She lifts her arms to the start position and counts off. The orchestra begins the introduction to "I Will Rejoice." The sound is pure and glorious. Harmony waves her arms like a fluttering bird about to take flight. Her love for the Lord is obvious; her enthusiasm, unharnessed. As the song concludes she offers one more shot for the team.

"That was wonderful! I'll see you back here on Sunday! Sing it just like that!"

Ken stands and walks toward the front of the church. Harmony spots him and makes her way off the podium to give him a hug. He approaches his parents and hands Mrs. Odrey the flowers. Mr. Odrey smiles. Harmony looks touched.

"Oh, honey, now that's what I'm talkin' about! Forgiveness, reconciliation, restoration and the love-love. That's my Jesus! That's what He's all about. And that's what we're supposed to be all about, too!"

❦ ❦ ❦

It is about eight o'clock in the evening when Winnie and Casey enter the elevator in the lobby of the Hit Maker Music building. They make their way to the top floor and exit the elevator. Casey places her key in the lock. It won't turn.

"My key doesn't work!"

"Here, let me try, maybe the lock is just swollen."

"And what would have caused that? All the rainstorms we've been experiencing indoors?"

Winnie tries, but to no avail, and hands the keys back to Casey. Angered, she throws them against the wall.

"Bert has had the locks changed. It's all part of his power play to take over my company!"

"C'mon Casey, let's just go. I'll get this straightened out tomorrow."

Livid, Casey shouts, "Has Bert had a freakin' lobotomy?"

Casey's phone rings.

"Hello? Yes, hi, Annie."

"Casey, you've got to call Erika Marie's dad. He wants out of his contract with us."

"What? Why?"

Casey turns to Winnie and inquires, "Can I call a client?"

Winnie says, "No. Not until you are reinstated."

"Well I better get reinstated! One of my most successful artists wants out of her contract!"

Annie continues.

"Her dad says all the negative press is affecting things: the affiliation with drunk driving and disregard for the law. 'You're a *convict* now!' His words, not mine."

"Are you serious?"

"He says two sponsors are threatening to drop out of the tour. They're getting pressure from their patrons. You know, for supporting a company whose CEO is—"

"I get it."

"—I'm so sorry, Casey."

As she ends the call, Casey is infuriated and nearly out of her mind. She addresses Winnie.

"I need to have a meeting with everyone. My employees, my artists, their managers and agents, our sponsors for the tours. Everyone. You've got to arrange it. Immediately! I've worked too hard to lose everything."

"Let me drive you home. I'll see what I can do."

Casey spends the rest of the evening at home, coming up with a strategy to resolve her situation. She paces the floor, takes a two-hour bubble bath and for most of the night lies in bed staring at the ceiling. Even after a couple glasses of wine she remains restless and finds it impossible to sleep.

As the sun rises, she throws on her jogging suit and begins running on her treadmill. After an hour, she hits the showers. As she towels off she calls Winnie to see if she's arranged the meeting yet.

"Casey, it's Sunday. I promise you, I'm on it, first thing Monday morning. Meet me at church. You're putting in hours at the Eagle's Nest this afternoon anyway. Just meet me. I'm worried about you."

Casey is silent and immersed in her own thoughts.

"Casey?"

"Yeah, I'm here. Okay, whatever."

As Casey enters the back of the church, the service is just about to start. Winnie motions her to come to the fourth row down front.

Casey slides in and is tightly surrounded by Jazzy, Olivia and Alex. Winnie, Nick, Ken, Phyllis and the Odreys complete the pew. Harmony conducts a gloriously executed chorus of "This is the Day."

Arriving late, Rachel makes her way into the pew. Casey makes eye contact but doesn't immediately recognize her. Harmony and the choir end the song and she turns beaming to see Casey's response. Casey, tightly wedged in her seat, sits expressionless as Pastor Joel takes the podium.

"This morning I'd like to talk to you about sheep."

Casey leans over to Winnie and whispers, "Oh, now there's a hot topic!"

Winnie gives her the eye as Pastor Joel continues.

"Have you ever wondered why Jesus is often referred to in Scripture as the good shepherd? Let me explain. Much like us, sheep are very dumb, stubborn animals. In fact, and again much like us, even though they may not realize their need for help, direction and guidance, they are totally dependent on their shepherd for every need they have. Sheep can be standing right next to a stream and thirst to death unless the shepherd leads them to drink. Have you ever had a thirst for something you found impossible to quench? And if sheep fall over, it is impossible for them to get back up unless the shepherd assists them. Have you ever been knocked down so much you feel too weak to try again?"

Casey becomes slightly more curious.

"When lambs are young they have a tendency to wander off from the flock, just as we have a tendency wander away from God's ways and His highest and best will for our lives. Lambs can become lost, maimed or even killed by predators."

Casey listens with attentive interest.

"The shepherd will watch and warn a straying lamb, but a lamb that tends to go astray often won't heed his warning. Knowing the dangers of going astray, out of a loving desire to protect and care for his flock, the shepherd breaks the lamb's leg."

Casey grimaces.

"The shepherd doesn't want to hurt the lamb, only to protect it. While the lamb's leg is healing, he carries the lamb next to his heart. By the time the leg has mended, the lamb is so dependent on the shepherd that it will never leave his side."

Casey looks stung. With a furrowed brow, she gazes up at the stained glass window of Jesus holding the lamb.

"Jesus is the good shepherd because He will go to any extent necessary to care for us, to protect us and to meet our every need. He loves us with a love that never changes and never fails. And He wants the very best for us."

Rachael looks at Casey, who remains pensive. Harmony catches Casey's eye and smiles at her. Jazzy looks up at Casey and tries to quietly impart some wisdom.

"Baaaaaaaahhh!"

Casey motions her to be quiet.

"That's how a lamb goes, case you didn't know," whispers Jazzy.

🐑🐑🐑

As church adjourns, several people make their way over to the Eagle's Nest. Today is the third Sunday of the month. That's the day when potential foster parents and even those looking for permanent adoptions come for a visit. All the children are dressed immaculately and on their best behavior, each one hoping that today will be the day when they get picked to become part of a real family.

There's a table filled with an array of finger foods and two large punch bowls of lemonade. Harmony, Ken, Nick, Winnie, the Odreys, some other seniors and Casey are given the assignment of serving food and co-hosting. The children mingle with about a dozen couples.

Phyllis makes rounds and attempts to match make. Alex, Olivia and Jazzy stick together and go from couple to couple with Alex making the introductions. Alex and Olivia are dressed in their church clothes; Jazzy wears baseball garb. Casey brings out a tray of sandwiches and notices Alex with Olivia and Jazzy in tow approaching the Kirks, a preppy-looking, interracial couple in their mid-thirties.

"Hi," says Alex.

"Hi," the Kirks say in unison.

"My name is Alex and these are my sisters, Olivia and Jazzy."

"Hi," says Jazzy as Olivia smiles shyly and waves.

"We want to be adopted together," Alex boldly proclaims.

"That's so sweet," replies Mrs. Kirk.

"Unfortunately we're only looking for one new family member," adds Mr. Kirk.

"But you keep looking. Whoever gets you three will certainly be lucky," said Mrs. Kirk.

Disappointed, Alex mumbles, "That's what everybody always says."

Casey, overhearing the entire exchange, seems troubled as she picks up an empty tray and watches the threesome. A flashback of Casey's early years scrolls through her memory like an old home movie. At nine years old, she sits on a bench inside an orphanage. Potential parents interacting with many of the other children surround her. She continues to sit alone and observe, hoping that someone will want her. She recalls all the pain, the loneliness and the rejection. She takes the empty tray she holds into the kitchen and wipes the tears she fights desperately to control.

🐾🐾🐾

After all the guests leave, Casey has promised to conduct an art class in the backyard. Ten children ages five to twelve, as well as Alex, Olivia, Jazzy, the Odreys, Ken and Harmony all stand behind easels. Casey goes from child to child offering input. Nick and Winnie observe. Olivia paints a beautiful flower. Alex puts the finishing touches on a very detailed robot. Jazzy frantically flings vibrant paint colors onto her canvas.

Her rendering is very colorful and abstract. The execution of her artistry seems to be enhanced by her perpetual tongue movements. She wears a baseball glove on one hand and has her paintbrush in the other. In deep concentration, she wildly paints with complete abandon.

Casey carefully examines all the work in progress, and seems to be particularly drawn to Jazzy's effort. She reviews it with uncommon interest, astounded by Jazzy's intensity and freeform style. Maybe it's the color combination. Maybe it's the textures and tones. Or perhaps it's that she wonders how anyone could possibly paint with one hand while wearing a baseball mitt on the other.

Chapter 12

At Hit Maker Music, Sunday is no different from any other day for Bert. He sits at his desk overwhelmed with trying to fill Casey's shoes. Jack enters, carrying several mockups for gospel music logos. Bert seems surprised to see Jack at the offices on a weekend.

"Jack, what are you doing here on a Sunday?"

"I have a surprise for you! Worked on this for the last several days!"

Jack holds up several versions of gospel label logos.

"What are these?"

"I know you want to open a gospel label, so I took the liberty of doing some logo mockups for you."

"But Jack, you know Casey isn't interested in that."

Jack smiles deviously and hands Bert a slip of paper and a set of keys.

"I also had the code and the locks changed so she couldn't get in and sabotage the new direction we've decided to take."

"Jack you shouldn't have done that. Besides, my signature is required to make any changes like that."

"Yes, I know," Jack replies smugly. "I forged it perfectly."

Bert shakes his head and gives Jack a look of displeasure.

"You overstepped your authority, Jack. I see this as a deliberate act of insubordination. See that it doesn't happen again."

"Okay, Bert, but you're in charge now. I see this as your opportunity. I'd give it some thought if I were you."

With that, Jack leaves the mockups and exits. Thoughtfully, Bert stares out his office window.

Following the art class at the Eagle's Nest, the children begin to put away their supplies and move their work inside to dry. Casey addresses Phyllis as they all make their way back inside.

"May I speak with you?"

"Of course. Why don't we go into my office?"

Casey follows Phyllis down the hallway and sits in a chair across from her desk.

"How did Alex end up here?"

"His father was a professor and his mom was a pediatrician. Both parents were killed in a car accident and we were unable to locate any surviving relatives."

"How long has he been here?"

"Two years."

"What about Olivia and Jazzy?"

"Olivia's mother died of a drug overdose. We don't know anything about her father."

"Why doesn't she speak?"

"We've had her tested and there's no physiological reason. Muteness is not uncommon in abused or abandoned children. But she'll come around. Jazzy's mother died of cancer and her father, or should I say, sperm donor, has no parental rights and is in prison."

Casey appears to be in deep thought. Phyllis breaks her concentration.

"Why do you ask?"

"I was just curious. Thanks, Phyllis."

"Where are you from, Casey?"

Casey stands to leave.

"I prefer not to talk about my private life."

"I didn't mean to intrude. I apologize."

"No apology necessary."

"Will you be coming to church next Sunday? Afterwards is our annual picnic."

Seemingly preoccupied, Casey half-heartedly responds, "I don't know … um … probably not for church. I may drop by afterwards."

"Yes, of course. Well, maybe we'll see you sometime during the week as well."

"Yeah, maybe. Probably. One more question. What is your annual budget?"

"Seven hundred thousand."

Apparent that her mind's wheels are turning, she repeats what Phyllis has said.

"Seven hundred thousand."

And with that Casey leaves the Eagle's Nest.

※ ※ ※

Casey and Winnie stand outside the front door of the Hit Maker Music offices reading a piece of paper with the new code. They disarm the alarm and enter.

"I just can't believe that Bert would try to keep me out of my own office. Why would he do that?"

As they walk down the hallway Winnie responds, "I didn't speak to him. Annie just gave me the code. But you should be able to straighten a lot of this out when you have your meeting of the minds."

"Yeah, again thanks for making that happen, Wins. I really look forward to having an audience with all of them. The files I need to pick up are in Bert's office."

As they enter Bert's office, Casey stumbles over several easels with different logos for a gospel label. Casey picks up one of the mockups.

"Look at this! Now Bert's trying to go over my head and open a gospel label. I gave an emphatic *no* to that idea. What's wrong with him? Winnie, I'm dying here. Please get me reinstated."

"I'm doing everything I know to do, Casey. You have to be patient."

Casey retrieves the files she needs and muses over a platinum record of Erika Marie's as they retrace their steps back down the hallway and toward the entrance.

"As an example, Erika Marie here. Remember I told you that her dad has decided he wants to terminate her contract with me because I'm a bad example? 'A *convict*.'"

"Yes."

"Well, tonight she has a big concert in Charlotte. I should be there!"

"We'll get things straightened out, Casey. It's complicated and takes time, but we'll get there."

※ ※ ※

With loyal fans trying to make their way to the stadium for Erika Marie's evening concert, traffic in Charlotte is at a standstill. Reporters swarm like flies outside her dressing room, waiting their turns for a pre-show interview. One reporter fires off a comment.

"Erika, you must feel a little uncomfortable endorsing Students Against Drunk Driving campaigns all over the country that are sponsored by your own record company, when its president—"

Bud interrupts. "Look, we believe in what we do. And to show how disgusted we are with Casey Alliston, we are not re-upping our contract with Hit Maker Music."

Erika angrily responds.

"I think we all make mistakes! I need to get ready for my concert. You'll need to leave now. Thank you for coming."

Erika gives Bud a look as he escorts the reporters away from her dressing room. Bud continues to try to do damage control by kissing up to them. Erika slams her dressing room door and texts Casey.

I wish you could be here. I miss you. xoxo, E.

❧ ❧ ❧

The wicker table in Casey's sunroom is filled with Chia pets in all sizes and shapes. Home Shopping Network boxes in various sizes are stacked everywhere.

With her hair tied up on top of her head, Casey wears a green facial mask and sits hidden behind boxes at her desk, making calculations on her computer. The wall clock shaped like a music note says it's 8:15 p.m.

Casey receives Erika's text. She is visibly moved and although she knows she's not permitted to speak with any of her artists until pending issues are resolved, no one mentioned anything about texting. She returns a message.

I miss you, too, Kiddo. Hit it out of the park tonight! xoxo, C.

Casey spends the rest of the evening working on her calculations. The evening passes quickly. The next time she looks at her wall clock, it's 2:30 a.m.

She prints out a twenty-page document of computations and places them in a file folder. She shuts down her laptop, stands slowly and stretches long and wide. Then, the moment she has long awaited has finally arrived. She claps her hands together twice and her newly installed HSN clapper turns off the lights. She smiles with immense satisfaction. Officially exhausted, she fumbles in the darkness and retires to her bedroom for the night.

Chapter 13

It's 8:30 on Sunday morning when Casey is awakened by her phone ringing. She makes her way out from under a mound of covers, unstraps her facelift gear and fumbles for the phone. Still half asleep, she answers.
"Hello?"
Alex, who is dressed and ready for church, timidly addresses her.
"Casey, it's Alex."
Casey, becoming more alert, sits up in bed.
"Alex, what is it? Are you alright?"
"I feel like I'm going to throw up."
"Well did you tell Phyllis or Harmony?"
"I'm not sick. I'm scared."
"Scared? About what?"
"I'm singing my first solo today. That's why I'm calling you. To see if you have any advice that might help me?"
She tries to think fast, as fast as anyone is able having just awakened.
"Well, what I've always found that works is to pretend everyone in the audience is wearing their underwear on their heads."
Alex laughs.
"That's pretty funny, Casey! I think my butterflies are better already. Are you coming to hear me?"
"Ah, actually Alex, I wasn't planning on coming to church. I was coming over afterwards for the picnic."
Disappointed, and followed by a long pause, Alex responds, "Oh."
Detecting the letdown, Casey attempts to recover. "But that was before I knew you were doing a solo. I'm on my way. I wouldn't miss it! Look for me!"
Alex beams, "Thanks, Casey!"
Casey readies herself in record time and arrives at church, meeting Phyllis as she runs up the stairs. Casey hands Phyllis a file folder.
"Good morning, Casey."

"Good morning, Phyllis. Alex wants me to hear him sing."

Phyllis smiles.

"Take a look at my proposal and see what you think. It's a way to purchase the building you're in and retire the debt in five years."

Phyllis fights back the tears.

"I've also enclosed an offer to put on a benefit concert to raise capital. With a few name artists I believe we could put a pretty big dent in your annual budget."

Phyllis throws her arms around Casey and then responds.

"But I don't think the woman who owns our building will sell it."

"Sure she will. She wants to buy the building her office is in."

Phyllis looks curious.

"I own that one," Casey says.

Phyllis is obviously overwhelmed and starts to make another comment as Casey's phone rings.

"Hello?"

"Hi, Casey. It's Annie."

"Hi Annie. What's up?"

"Casey there's been some really weird things going on."

"Yeah, I know. Listen, we'll straighten it all out this week at the meeting. In the meantime, Alex, this great little nine-year-old guy I've met, is about to sing his first solo at church. He needs me to be there for support. I want to hear more, but I really have to run. I'll call you later. Bye."

Annie holds the phone out in front of her face and stares at it.

"Children? Church? Who are you and what have you done with my boss?"

Phyllis, still teary-eyed, gives Casey a big bear hug before they enter the sanctuary. The congregation finishes the song, "Wonderful Peace," as they make their way down front. They sit with Winnie, Nick, the Odreys, Ken and Jazzy. A sixty-member, robed children's choir is on stage. Alex holds a microphone. Olivia and two other ballet dancers are dressed in long white, flowing gowns. Harmony approaches the podium.

"This morning we have a special song from our children's music ministry. It's entitled, 'He's a Great Big God.'"

As the introduction to "He's a Great Big God" begins, Alex looks petrified and is taking deep breaths. Suddenly, he looks out over the congregation. Although only in his mind, everyone is wearing underwear on their heads.

Confidently, he begins to sing. Olivia dances like an angel. As Casey listens, everyone in her pew watches her as she watches the kids. When she feels them looking at her and turns their way, they simultaneously look away from her and back at the kids. At the conclusion of the piece Casey is the first to her feet and applauds wildly. She gives Alex a thumbs up. He grins from ear to ear.

It's a perfect afternoon for a picnic at the neighborhood park. Everyone sits at picnic tables enjoying the massive quantity of food. Harmony sits next to Ken and talks his ear off.

Casey takes pictures of all of the activities. Winnie pushes the kids on the swings. A football spirals through the air as Alex catches a pass from Nick. Phyllis pushes the Odreys on the swings. A frisbee flies through the air and Olivia does a ballet move, then catches it. Casey puts her camera down to play catch with the kids. Alex tackles Jazzy. Jazzy tackles Casey. Jazzy winds up and throws a pitch to Casey. As the ball lands in Casey's glove she removes the glove, acting like Jazzy's pitch burned a hole in her hand. Casey faces a tree and begins to count as the kids scatter for a game of hide and seek. Casey turns from the tree.

"Ready or not, *here I come!*"

As she begins to look for the kids, her cell phone rings. She answers it and continues to look for the kids. Suddenly she stops and drops to her knees.

"Oh my God!"

Casey makes it to Northside Hospital in record time. Immediately, she locates Bert's doctor and he gives her the update.

"It was a massive stroke."

Casey frantically makes her way to the ICU. Somberly she sits by Bert's bedside. He is unconscious. Tubes and monitors are an ominous presence.

After several hours, the doctor suggests she should go home and get some rest.

"It's too soon to make any determination. The next 48 hours is critical. Get some rest."

Casey arrives home and decides to occupy her mind by doing something productive. She goes into her dark room and develops some of her pictures.

Winnie joins her.

As Casey manipulates the developing fluid, they see a beautiful action shot coming into focus. It's a picture of Alex throwing a pass. Casey removes it and hangs it on a wire. She hangs others along side, including Jazzy concentrating on throwing a pitch, Olivia doing a cartwheel and the Odreys on the swing set.

"In consideration of Bert's condition, I need to call an emergency meeting with the Board of Directors to vote on reinstating me immediately."

"I already took care of it. Your meeting is at ten tomorrow morning."

"Thanks, Wins."

Casey turns on the light and wipes down her equipment. She's pensive.

"You're really worried about Bert, aren't you?"

"Yeah, we've had our differences and all, but Bert gave me my start. The whole reason I believed I could build a record company is because Bert told me I could. We've always sparred with each other and gotten on each other's last nerve. But seeing him lying there so lifeless is just really tough."

Casey chokes back the tears. "I don't want anything to happen to him. I really don't."

"I know."

※ ※ ※

Over at Hit Maker Music, Jack has already called an emergency meeting. Seated in the conference room are Paul Boehlert, Ruth Bayslow, Erika Marie, Bud, two concert sponsors and several other board members. Jack begins the meeting.

"Thank you all for coming. As you know, Bert has had a stroke. In Casey's absence, I have worked hand in hand with him. I know we're all scheduled to meet with Casey tomorrow. But I felt it in the best interest of the company and its future that we meet now."

"Jack, I thought Casey would be here," says Paul.

"When you all hear what I have to say you'll understand why I felt it best to meet without her. Hit Maker Music has always been known for great music, great artists and taking the moral high road. We do drug tests on employees; we test our artists and band members. We have sponsored anti-drug and anti-drinking campaigns in schools. The company has built a sterling reputation. Then Casey's face is splashed all over the news for drunk driving."

The board members look uncomfortable. Paul responds.

"Jack, it was an error in judgment that she is rectifying. In fact, in most states, she wouldn't have even been considered over the limit. Anyone who knows Casey knows she rarely even drinks."

"Yes Paul, but it was an error in judgment that has caused two of Erika's concert sponsors to threaten to drop out of Erika's tour and has made her dad not want to re-up her contract with Hit Maker Music. We're talking an earning potential of millions in the toilet."

The sponsors nod their heads in agreement. Bud looks stoic but remains silent. Erika seems unusually perturbed.

"We can only assume there will be more incidents like this to follow where it affects our bottom line. I know Casey is meeting with you tomorrow for the express purpose of being reinstated. I suggest you keep her in a non-threatening, non-decision-making role where she flies under the radar. I propose that you think about the company first. I suggest that you consider appointing me to run the company. We need to have massive press coverage that assures our patrons we have a no-tolerance rule for breaking the law. This will rally everyone back to supporting us. We will continue to be role models!"

Jack turns to address Bud. "In fact, Bud, if you will agree to stay on with us, I think we could offer you a sizable signing bonus."

Bud makes no comment. Jack addresses the sponsors.

"Guys, how would your companies feel about what I've proposed?"

They nod affirmatively. Jack stands.

"Paul. Board members. I will leave you to discuss this. I can do this job and restore our good name. I think you can understand why this proposal needed to occur before the meeting with Casey. Again, we are talking millions in lost revenue by reinstating her. This is not what is best for Hit Maker Music."

Chapter 14

It is the day she's been waiting for! Her turn to have her say before the Board of Directors and be reinstated as captain of her ship. She is confident, and with Winnie by her side, it seems a sure thing. As Casey and Winnie enter the conference room, Paul and the board members are seated.

"Good morning, everyone. Thank you all for coming. In consideration of Bert's condition and because I am making restitution according to plan, I'd like to be reinstated immediately."

Everyone is mute and looks uncomfortable. Casey looks at Winnie. Paul clears his throat and begins speaking on behalf of the group.

"Casey, yesterday Jack called a meeting with the Board of Directors, Bud, Erika and a couple of your sponsors."

"*Jack?*" Casey shouts.

In an attempt to calm her down, Winnie grabs Casey's forearm, encouraging her to hear Paul out.

"You've gotten so much negative press and it has the potential to really affect our bottom line. We think it is in the best interest of Hit Maker Music that you continue to fly under the radar and that your participation be kept to a minimum."

Casey looks horrified and cannot contain her displeasure.

"You met behind my back? This is my company! I made a mistake, and I have paid dearly for it!"

Winnie joins in the battle.

"Paul when we set this meeting, you said that reinstating Casey was a mere formality."

"Yes, but Jack enlightened us on some very valid issues."

"Jack is a conniving little backstabber!" Casey replies.

Down the hall, Jack sits at his desk, eavesdropping on his intercom. Annie enters, snatches his intercom off of his desk and exits.

"We have made the decision that Jack will run the day to day operations until otherwise notified," Paul states.

The board members remain mute and uncomfortable. They avoid eye contact with Casey.

"Winnie, you've got to do something," pleads Casey.

Winnie confronts Paul.

"Paul, clearly, this entire meeting was sabotaged. This is nothing short of mutiny!"

"We feel that this decision is in the best interest of our artists and the future of the company. Casey you may come and go as you please," Paul states authoritatively.

Casey and Winnie stand to exit.

"You're making a terrible mistake," Casey says emphatically.

"This fight's not over, Paul," underscores Winnie.

The board members look ashamed. As Casey and Winnie enter the elevator, Casey is visibly upset and falls against the back wall. Winnie tries to comfort her. Casey turns to Winnie, sinks into her arms and sobs. The elevator opens. People waiting to enter stare as Casey continues to sob.

Casey says in a muffled tone, "Please, Winnie. Tell me we can fix this. Tell me it's not over."

People stare and begin to talk. Winnie whispers to Casey.

"Casey, we've reached our destination. You've got to let go of me. Onlookers think we're breaking up."

Casey releases her and puts on sunglasses. They exit with military precision.

As they leave the building Winnie assures Casey.

"I will go to work on this immediately. I believe they have overstepped their authority in fully circumventing you."

"You're the best, Wins. Thank you."

"I'll call you later with my findings."

"Okay, remember that tonight I'm taking the kids out for Olivia's birthday."

"Okay."

※ ※ ※

The Odreys, Harmony and Ken put the finishing touches on dressing Alex, Olivia and Jazzy to celebrate Olivia's birthday with Casey at the Fabulous Fox Theatre.

Casey picks them up in her limo. As they pull up to the Fox the children are in awe. The Fox is stunning. More than a century old and recently restored, the theatre's interior reflects the finest architecture of the period. Upon entering, Casey instructs the kids to look upward. The ceiling appears to be a star-sprayed midnight sky. Casey has arranged for fourth-row center seats.

As the ballet begins, Casey enjoys watching the faces of the children. Olivia is especially mesmerized.

She sits on the edge of her seat and studies every move, every jump. She examines each costume and every set change as though there will be a test to follow. In fact, Olivia is so completely engaged that even Alex and Jazzy become distracted and begin watching her scrutinize every detail of this spectacular presentation. At its conclusion, Olivia jumps to her feet and applauds until her little hands turn hot pink.

Following the performance, Casey instructs the driver to take them to the Buckhead Diner.

Casey and the kids are escorted to a white linen-draped table. In the center of the table is a beautifully decorated birthday cake containing three prominently displayed ballerinas and eight candles. The waitress lights the candles and the entire restaurant joins in singing, "Happy Birthday." Olivia blows out her candles with a little help from her friends. Excitedly, Olivia turns to Casey and whispers, "When I grow up I'm going to dance just like those dancers we saw!"

Casey, stunned and wide-eyed, tears up at Olivia's words. Alex and Jazzy give each other a high five.

"Oh, my goodness, Olivia, you spoke!" exclaimed Casey.

Alex grins broadly and responds.

"She had something to say!"

Jazzy gives Olivia two thumbs up and hugs her. Olivia giggles. On their drive back to the Eagle's Nest, they prepare a surprise presentation to announce Olivia's breakthrough. They enter the living room area and Casey summons everyone.

"Hello! Hello! Phyllis! Mr. and Mrs. Odrey! Everyone! Hurry!"

Within seconds the area is filled with anxious onlookers. Casey gives Olivia the nod.

"Olivia?"

There is a long pause as everyone anxiously awaits whatever it is they've been beckoned to experience. Then, in her own way, Olivia unveils her surprise.

"We're home!" Olivia quietly announces with great enthusiasm.

Everyone laughs and then bursts into applause. Alex and Olivia thank Casey for all the fun of the evening and scamper off.

"Okay, see you guys later," says Casey as she prepares to leave.

Everyone else disperses except for Jazzy, who follows Casey to the door.

"Casey?"

Casey turns and bends down to her eye level. Jazzy holds Casey's face with both hands.

"Casey, when Olivia blew out her candles, I made a wish, too!"

"You did? Can you do that?"

"Yep."

"Well then, what did you wish for?"

"I wished that you was my Mommy."

Jazzy hugs and kisses Casey then runs off. Casey tears up and looks stung as she watches Jazzy exit.

Her memory takes her back to her orphanage experience.

She is nine years old, kneeling by her bedside, praying and asking God to send her a Mommy and Daddy.

She open her eyes, wipes away the tears, and turns to leave. She is so preoccupied, she collides with Winnie just outside the door.

"Casey, what's the matter?" inquires Winnie.

"Nothing. Really, it's nothing."

Winnie puts her hand on Casey's shoulder.

"Casey, obviously it's not nothing."

Casey pulls away and says, "I wish I'd never come to this place."

"Casey, tell me—"

"I have to go, Wins."

Casey hurriedly exits.

She arrives home and slowly walks around her living room examining all the landscape pictures that Jazzy cited on her first visit. She goes into her dark room and gathers up some of the pictures she's taken with the kids. She comes back into the living room, begins taking some of the landscape shots out of their frames and replaces them with the new action shots of the kids.

The buzzer from the lobby interrupts her. The doorman announces that Winnie is in the lobby. Casey flags her up.

As Casey opens the door she says immediately, "Wins, I owe you an apology. I'm sorry I ran off like that."

"It's okay. But can you tell me what happened?"

"Jazzy told me that when Olivia blew out her birthday candles that she made a wish. She wished that I would be her Mommy."

Winnie looks empathetically at Casey.

"As you know, I was brought up in a home similar to the Eagle's Nest, only not as nice. I never even knew who my mom and dad were. Being at the Eagle's Nest has unearthed so many painful memories. All those times when adults would come for a visit and I'd just hope and pray someone would pick me. But it never happened. Watching Alex, Olivia and Jazzy approach every person on campus, one by one, telling them how great they are and knowing that they are hoping so hard that someone will pick them. It's excruciating to watch … to remember. And so when Jazzy actually said those words to me, it was devastatingly personal. It tore me out of the frame."

Winnie reaches out and hugs Casey as Casey fights back the tears.

"Can I offer you something to think about?"

"Okay," she murmurs sheepishly.

"I know you struggle with God and the Bible. But in the Bible it says that God allows us to be afflicted so that we might help others in the time of their affliction. Who better to empathize, encourage and love on these kids than you?"

Casey seems pensive and then responds unconvincingly, "Yeah, I suppose I get what you're saying."

After Winnie leaves, Casey decides to walk over to the hospital to check on Bert. She sits at his beside for a while. There is still no change. She touches his hand and looks at him, so helpless, so lifeless.

Chapter 15

The sign outside the church says, *Tonight: A Concert to Remember to Benefit the Eagle's Nest.* The advertising, press coverage and marketing for the event have gone splendidly. The auditorium is packed to overflowing.

The hair and makeup room is buzzing. Casey enters wearing a headset and carrying a clipboard. She speaks to one of the makeup artists.

"Have you seen Harmony? I need to go over a few notes here."

"No, I haven't."

She asks the same question of one of the hairdressers.

"Have you?"

"I do hair, Casey," she says playfully. "What would make you think I had seen Harmony? Nobody in our field has seen Harmony for at least twenty years!"

A lone woman trying to hide behind her broom sweeps hair from the floor. Casey addresses her.

"Excuse me?"

The woman pretends not to hear her.

"Excuse me?"

The woman turns around, revealing her identity. It's Rachael, Winnie's client.

"Rachael? What are you doing here?"

Timidly she replies, "I'm apprenticing at a hair studio. I'm working on getting my certificate in cosmetology."

"That's great Rachael. Good for you. Congratulations! Have you seen Harmony?"

"No, not for a while."

Casey exits and then returns to address Rachael.

"Really, Rachael. Congratulations."

Rachael is surprised, but is beaming.

Casey walks down several hallways and peeks in door after door. Finally she opens one where she finds Harmony sitting alone, tears streaming down her face and in prayer. Casey sits quietly until Harmony opens her eyes.

"What's the matter?" Casey asks.

"Oh nothing. I was just thanking God for you and praying about the concert."

"Why were you crying?"

"Oh, sometimes when you talk to God, Casey, you can just be overcome with tears of joy! He's so good the way He so tenderly loves us and meets all of our needs."

Casey is respectful and listens intently.

"Take you for instance. See, you think you came into our lives because you owed the state some community service hours. I think we prayed to God for help to meet our needs and here you are!"

"Hmmm ... interesting perspective. Harmony, do you ever ask God for anything for yourself?"

"Yes, girl. Although I do think Ken is close to popping the question, I ask the Lord to send me a husband at least every few hours. And I watch Dr. Phil to learn everything I can about relationships!"

"'How's that workin' for ya?' I love when he says that! 'How's that workin' for ya!' Direct and to the point. I love bottom-liners!"

"You watch him, too?"

"Love him!"

Casey springs to her feet and grabs Harmony by the wrist.

"C'mon girl. I gotta treat for you."

Casey drops Harmony off in the hair and makeup room and then heads to the sound booth. After putting the finishing touches on her lighting and sound cues, she's ready for showtime. Her adrenaline is pumping. She communicates with Nick and Winnie who man the follow spots on either side of the auditorium. The orchestra tunes up and Casey readies herself to launch the evening. From her perch, acting as the announcer, she begins.

"Good evening and welcome to *A Night to Remember*. Thank you for coming. And now if you will, please put your hands together and join me in welcoming our Mistress of Ceremonies for the evening. She's a Grammy award-winning singer, a much sought after speaker and author. You can find her hosting television broadcasts and conferences that positively affect the lives of young people. She's a wife and a mom, too! Put you're your hands together for the one and only CeCe Winans!"

Everyone stands, applauds and cheers as CeCe takes the stage.

"Thank you, everybody. I'm so pleased to be part of such a worthy cause! Your presence here tonight says you feel the same way, too."

The audience bursts into applause once again.

"We've got a great lineup tonight that we know you will enjoy. So without further adieu, let's introduce our first artist of the evening. She's a Grammy award-winning singer, has multi-platinum albums, and is a mom and wife to another of our favorites, Tim McGraw. But one very special detail that you may or may not know, is that both she and her husband, Tim, are adopted, which makes their appearance here tonight all the more meaningful. Singing 'The Hard Way,' and 'I Will Have Loved,' ladies and gentlemen please give a warm welcome to Faith Hill!"

Faith sings to a delighted audience.

CeCe returns to the stage to welcome the next artist.

"Next, we have someone who's been a longtime friend of mine as well as a good friend to Harmony Jones, the director of the Christ Community Church Choir. She has recorded 25 records, had Top 5 songs on the radio and sung numerous times on The Billy Graham Crusades. Please make welcome Babbie Mason. Babbie sings 'I Can 'Never Get Enough' and 'The Only Hope.'"

Babbie Mason makes a heartfelt connection with the crowd. As Babbie leaves the stage, Harmony Jones, who needs no introduction, walks to the microphone sporting a short, bouncy haircut, no glasses, flawless makeup and wearing a long, sequin gown. She takes the microphone from its stand and makes an announcement.

"For anyone wondering, I am Harmony Jones—yes I am—the music director for the Christ Community Church choir."

Ken's jaw drops to the floor. Mr. and Mrs. Odrey smile and nudge their son. Casey beams broadly and gives Harmony two thumbs up. The entire audience applauds enthusiastically as the choir files into the choir loft.

Harmony takes center stage, does a count off and the orchestra begins to play the intro to "All in Favor." The choir does a magnificent job and continues by singing, "Can I Get an Amen?'" At the conclusion, the audience gives them a standing ovation.

CeCe returns to the podium to announce the next artist.

"She's a five time Grammy award winner, been Top 5 on radio more times than we can count and is also an best-selling author. Let's give it up for Wynonna, who sings, 'Love Works Every Time,' 'The Great Exchange,' and 'Teach Me How to Love Like That.'"

The concert is in full swing, and the beautiful music continues.

"Next please show your love for Faith Hill's husband: the gifted, multi-talented, the one and only Tim McGraw singing, 'Luckiest Man Alive.' and 'This Love.'"

"And finally, she has a distinct voice known to untold millions that has earned her every award out there and then some. But she may be equally known for her kind and generous heart! Ladies and gentlemen, give it up for Martina McBride, who sings, 'Live in the Moment,' and 'All Roads Lead to You.'"

As the song ends, CeCe returns to the stage holding an oversized check. She makes a presentation to Phyllis who stands beside her.

"Phyllis Early is the director of the Eagle's Nest. Tonight's concert, along with corporate sponsorships, has raised a quarter of a million dollars for the Eagle's Nest!"

CeCe hands Phyllis the check. Phyllis is visibly overwhelmed. The congregation bursts into applause as Phyllis holds up the check in proud display. Cameras flash all over the auditorium. Phyllis takes the microphone.

"This event would never have happened were it not for one very hardworking, kind, and generous individual. Her name is Casey Alliston. Casey?"

Nick and Winnie force Casey to join Phyllis onstage as the audience gives another lengthy standing ovation. CeCe joins in the hug-fest and then everyone leaves her on the stage.

"Thank you, every one of you, for coming tonight, and for your support for the Eagle's Nest. I'd like to close our concert tonight by singing one last song, titled, 'Heart of a Child.'"

What a fitting end to a beautiful evening of love and music! Everyone jumps to their feet and gives one last, lengthy standing ovation.

"Thank you for coming everybody! God bless you, God bless the children and drive safely going home. Good night!"

🍋🍋🍋

The concert hall has cleared and the volunteers are breaking down the stage. Casey is still sitting in a pew with Jazzy asleep in her lap. Olivia lies asleep beside her. Alex helps Nick tear down stage equipment. Winnie and Phyllis are sitting in the pew in front of Casey and turn sideways to talk with her. Ruth (with her teacup poodle in tow) and her husband approach.

"Casey, what a marvelous evening. You keep up good work like this and we'll be giving you back your *Woman of the Year* plaque in no time."

"And reinstating me, right?"

Ruth seems uneasy and uncomfortable.

"In time, dear. All in time."

Casey disregards her ignorance.

"Well, thanks for coming."

Ruth and her husband leave as the Odreys, Ken and Harmony approach. The Odreys hug Casey.

"That was quite an evening, angel!" boasts Mr. Odrey.

"Thanks, Mr. O."

"It was wonderful, Casey," adds Mrs. Odrey.

"Thank you."

Casey gives Harmony the once-over.

"You are looking mah-va-lous dah-link!"

Casey teases Ken and the Odreys.

"Am I to assume the separation has been resolved?"

"As long as our son behaves, we're all good," exclaims Mr. Odrey.

"We're going dancing," says Mrs. Odrey.

"Now don't wear these two out by staying up too late," Casey says.

"We'll try not to, sweetie. We love you," says Mrs. Odrey.

"Love you, too."

"And we're proud of you, too," adds Mr. Odrey.

Winnie smiles and winks at Ken. He winks back as the Odreys, Ken and Harmony make their way to the dance hall.

"Well ladies, shall we get these sleeping beauties to bed?" Casey suggests.

Winnie picks up Olivia, Casey picks up Jazzy. Phyllis puts her arm around Casey and kisses her on the cheek as they take the sleeping beauties home to bed at the Eagle's Nest.

"You headed home?" asks Winnie.

"No, I'm still wired. Thought I'd swing by the hospital and see if there's any change with Bert."

Chapter 16

As Casey enters Bert's hospital room, he is fragile, but finally awake. Casey sits close to him. His ability to speak is slow and labored, but he insists.

"Please forgive me, Casey, for the tension between us."

"Bert, just lie still."

"I have to say this. I've always believed in you, but I've always felt like I was just a bystander. The truth of the matter is, I guess I was a little envious. Not that I wasn't proud of you. I have always been proud. I've always thought of you like a daughter."

Casey is moved.

"A daughter?" Casey responds.

Bert nods affirmatively and slowly reaches to take her hand. She gently clasps his hand.

"We're a lot alike you know."

"Bert, you probably should try to conserve your energy."

"You need to know these things, Casey. It's about Hit Maker Music. Do you have anything to record this?"

Casey looks troubled and pulls out her phone.

"My phone. Tell me when."

Bert nods for her to start. His speech is slow and labored.

"Jack alerted the media the night you were arrested. He made logos for a gospel label to try to usurp you. He's met with Bud, Erika and concert sponsors to convince them to leave Hit Maker Music. He also had the locks changed on our offices and did so without my knowledge or permission. He forged my signature, as well, which I believe is a felony. You need to be rid of him. He's poison. Look in our office safe. There are surveillance tapes of his comings and goings, with more than enough evidence to prosecute him."

Bert closes his eyes to rest. Casey stops recording.

"Thank you for telling me this Bert. Jack convinced the Board of Directors to put him in charge until further notice. What you have told me will be helpful. But there are some things I need to say to you, too."

Bert opens his eyes and looks at her.

"Bert, please forgive me. I was a hothead. I blamed you and judged you for things you didn't do. You gave me my start and I'll always be grateful to you for that. Really. I owe my success to you. I believed I could build a record company because you told me I could."

Casey breaks down in tears but tries to compose herself.

"You should try to rest now."

He ignores her suggestion and continues with strain and difficulty. Casey continues to hold his hand.

"Casey, learn from my mistakes. What matters in life is your family and your friends. That's what makes you rich and successful. I have a great family but I never had time for them. Now it's too late for me. Don't wait until it's too late for you, too."

"I promise you Bert. I will take your advice."

Not too weak to tease her, he says in a very meek voice, "Well, that'll be a first."

Casey smiles and wipes away a tear.

"You rest now."

She bends down, kisses his cheek and then exits.

※ ※ ※

Casey barely sleeps that night. The next morning she calls an emergency meeting with Winnie, Paul, her staff and the Board of Directors. Casey holds in her hand her phone recording and the surveillance tapes Bert told her he had stored in their office safe.

Casey begins, "I've called this meeting—"

Jack interrupts. "Actually, Casey, I'm the one who conducts the meetings around here."

"—Not today, Jack. Sit down."

Jack is taken aback and sits down. Everyone else remains silent and still.

"The temporary arrangement of having an incompetent, backbiting, disloyal surrogate at the helm of my company has to end today! I've paid for my mistake and it's time for me to resume my rightful place."

Holding up her evidence, she addresses Jack.

"Bert filled me in on all your attempts to discredit me and take over my company. I've got the evidence here and the evidence is clear."

"Got what? You got nothing!" Jacks blurts out.

"Jack, please. Let's not play dumb. It's unbecoming."

Jack looks guilty. Annie looks triumphant. The rest of the group watches intently.

"Calling the media to alert them about my arrest. Having the locks and the alarm code changed and forging Bert's signature to do it. Last I checked that is a felony. Getting the logos done for a gospel label that I had adamantly made clear I had no interest in. Trying to get sponsors to cancel their tour support and convincing Bud to leave the label. It was all to try to get rid of me so you could rise to the top!"

"You have no proof of these accusations! Just the muddy recollection of a dying old man."

Casey motions to Annie for a security tape.

"Jack, unfortunately for you, I have everything I need to prosecute you to the fullest extent of the law. You see Jack, long before you ever started working for me, I had video cameras installed so that disloyalty could be kept in check. We also have an airtight security system on our phones and computers. You and your actions have buried you!"

All the blood runs out of Jack's face.

"Leave now. Security will escort you out."

"I'll need to have time to clean out my desk."

"Sorry Jack, you have no desk."

A security guard enters and escorts Jack out. Everyone in the room is ashamed and stunned with her findings. She addresses Paul.

"Paul, take a vote."

"I make a motion to reinstate Casey as the CEO of Hit Maker Music."

"I second it," says Ruth.

"Can I get show of hands?"

"It's unanimous." The staff cheers!

Paul makes an offering. "Casey, on behalf of myself and the Board of Directors, I'd like to apologize to you for all the pain and angst we've caused you."

Casey smiles and says, "Thank you. I accept your apology."

The Board of Directors stands and leaves. Winnie congratulates Casey and leaves Casey to address her staff.

"Now, let's get back to making music, shall we?"

Casey walks down the hall to her office. She sits down at her desk and takes a long look at her beloved surroundings as though reconnecting with a long lost friend. She swivels her chair around to face the Atlanta skyline. It feels great to be back at the helm. And yet, she feels a new sense of real contentment. She recognizes that her heart has expanded to include people, places and things beyond work. She considers how this embryonic growth is still developing, and she knows that this newly discovered balance is as it should be. She checks her watch, takes it off and places it inside her top desk drawer. Rubbing her wrist as though calming a slight irritation, she is not quite conscious that for the first time ever, she is bothered by the constraint of time.

※ ※ ※

Although today has been marked as a day of jubilant celebration on several fronts, there's still more celebrating to do. It's Jazzy's birthday! Across town at the Eagle's Nest, Phyllis, Alex, Olivia, Harmony, Ken, the Odreys and others gather around Jazzy, who proudly wears her birthday hat. She has looked forward to turning six all year. They sing "The New Happy Birthday Song" as she blows out birthday candles on her cake. Everyone cheers.

After she opens a few presents and the cake has been served, the older children begin getting dressed and ready to leave for the county youth choir competition scheduled for this afternoon. Harmony is busy with many last-minute details. In orderly fashion, the kids in the youth choir file quietly onto the bus. The Christ Community Church bus is packed without even one seat to spare as Harmony stands at the front imparting equal amounts of cheerleading and performance instructions.

"Okay, everyone take a seat. We will be singing three songs at the competition. Save your voices until then! We want to bless everyone there! Just do your best and sing to the Lord with everything you've got!"

The bus pulls away just as Casey arrives. She waves to Harmony and the kids as they depart. As she makes her way up the sidewalk, she notices Jazzy, still wearing her birthday hat, is peering out the bay window. Jazzy begins to cry as she watches the bus pull away, hurt that she's been left behind. Casey enters and attempts to comfort her.

"Hey, why the tears, birthday girl?"

"Cause Olivia and Alex got to go on the bus and I didn't."

"Well, you're not in the youth choir yet. And anyway, if you were on the church bus then you couldn't come with me to a special place that I want to show you for your birthday surprise."

Jazzy brushes away her tears, beams and jumps up into Casey's arms. Casey sets her down and opens the front door. Walking together to the limo, they plop down in the backseat where Jazzy clings to Casey in a permanent hug. The driver, previously instructed as to their destination, heads toward Peachtree Dekalb Airport. As they pull into the main gate, the planes flying overhead captivate Jazzy. The limo drops them off at a private hanger where a King Air awaits.

"We get to ride in this?" Jazzy exclaims excitedly.

"We sure do!"

Jazzy looks out the window for the entire trip and asks a gazillion questions. Casey attempts to address them all but in the process wonders if one day Jazzy will compete with Harmony on the most words spoken in a day. In fact, the only time Jazzy takes a verbal hiatus is when she eats the snack Casey has arranged for her: shrimp cocktail, crackers, sparkling apple juice and gingersnaps for dessert.

After a short forty-five minute flight, they land at Jekyll Island. Casey, in true form, photographs every moment. First things first! They stroll down the sandy beach. Jazzy is wide-eyed as she drinks in all the new sights and sounds.

The ocean is emerald green with layers of blue, the color of Jazzy's jacket. The smell of salt air is refreshing and the sounds of waves rhythmically crashing against the sand are like a sweet lullaby. The seagulls fly overhead singing warm greetings and seem to wave as they soar past. Jazzy picks up shells and stuffs her pockets. She notices a sand crab scurrying across her path and squeals with excitement.

As though on cue, a school of dolphins dances about fifty feet from shore. Finally, in the distance and just at sunset, they see a lighthouse. Casey imposes on a passerby to take their picture in front of it. Powerful waves caress it, as its brilliant beacon of light rotates, shining broadly for anyone needing to find a safe course. Casey holds Jazzy tightly as they continue to admire the lighthouse.

"As long as you can see the light you can always find your way home, Jazzy."

Jazzy gently places her hands on Casey's cheeks and looks into her eyes.

"Casey, what time is it?"

Casey looks at her wrist and is shocked that she has forgotten her watch. She is amused.

"I don't know. It's hard to believe that I don't have the foggiest notion what time it is. Why?"

"Is it still my birthday?"

"Oh, yeah! It's definitely still your birthday! And I have more surprises for you!"

They walk back to the limo and are whisked away to the Inn by the Sea restaurant where they are escorted to a table overlooking the ocean. Casey gives Jazzy a tiny package to open. It's a miniature lighthouse. Casey shows her a button to press that makes the beacon light up. Jazzy turns it on and off a few times.

"Thank you, Casey!"

They order dinner and at its conclusion, the waiter brings a birthday cupcake with a number six candle lit for her to make her wish. Jazzy gleefully looks at her cupcake as other waiters and waitresses surround the table singing "Happy Birthday." Jazzy closes her eyes tightly, makes her wish, opens her eyes, smiles at Casey and then blows out the big number six. Everyone applauds.

🐚🐚🐚

The church bus pulls up to the curb at the Eagle's Nest and the exhausted youth choir begins to leave the bus. Casey and Jazzy pull up in the limo right behind them. Alex and Olivia run to hug Casey. Olivia attempts to console Jazzy.

"Sorry you couldn't come, Jazzy."

"It's okay, Olivia. I got to fly in a plane—a real plane—and see a real lighthouse and the ocean! It's kind of blue and kind of green!"

Olivia and Alex look surprised.

"How was the singing competition? Did you win anything?" Casey inquires.

"Yep. We got two ribbons," reports Alex.

"Congratulations. I'm really proud of you!" says Casey.

"Great job, Alex and Olivia! And I'm glad you found your way back home," Jazzy adds, clicking on and off the beacon on her miniature lighthouse. "If you ever get lost, you just gotta follow the light and you can always find your way home."

Chapter 17

It's the third Sunday of the month and once again potential parents drop by the Eagle's Nest to meet the children. Alex and Olivia are dressed in their Sunday best. Jazzy has on a T-shirt that says, *God Hears Even the Smallest Prayers*, with her normal baseball garb. The three stand before a visiting Caucasian couple in their early forties. As Alex initiates an introduction to the couple, Jazzy tosses her ball up in the air and catches it a few times.

"My name is Alex and these are my sisters, Olivia and Jazzy."

"Well isn't that nice," says the man.

Jazzy's ball comes down and taps the woman's shoulder. She's a little startled. Jazzy jumps a few steps away to retrieve the ball. The woman brushes herself off.

Slightly miffed, she remarks, "Oh, my. Well whoever gets all of you will certainly be lucky duckies."

The couple moves along to the next kids when Jazzy returns to the circle. Alex is infuriated and gives her a harsh reprimand.

"Look, Jazzy. Do you see how Olivia and I are dressed? Every week we go through this. When I point out that you're our sister too and we all want to be adopted together, they walk away."

Jazzy is wide-eyed and speechless.

"Do you know why?" Alex asks.

Timidly, Jazzy responds, "No."

"I'll tell you why! It's because you're always dressed like a little tomboy. You just hit that lady with your ball, Jazzy. What's your glove and ball even doing in here? Gloves and balls belong outside, not inside! How many times do you have to be reminded?"

Jazzy looks at her glove and ball and then back at Alex. He continues. "Why can't you cooperate instead of ruining everything?" Alex stomps out of the room and Jazzy begins to cry.

"I'm sorry, Olivia. I made a mistake."

Olivia looks at her empathetically but says nothing. Jazzy darts out of the room.

❦ ❦ ❦

Casey walks briskly down the steps outside Northside Hospital. Her cell phone rings and she answers it. Phyllis has called to tell her Jazzy has disappeared and asks if Casey has seen her. With a look of panic on her face, Casey slides into the backseat of her limo and tells her driver to hurry to the Eagle's Nest.

Casey arrives to see a police car in the front of the building. The Odreys, Ken, Harmony, Winnie, Alex, Olivia and other volunteers are crowded together on the sidewalk. Casey gets out of the limo and rushes to them. Nick is in uniform and instructs everyone.

"Jazzy has only been missing for about two hours so we can't file an official report yet. All we can do is spread out and look for her ourselves. Think of places she likes to go. Any place she could hide. Try anywhere that comes to mind."

Winnie hands out photos of Jazzy and the crowd begins to disperse in all directions. Winnie and Nick then turn to Casey and surround her with hugs. She is obviously worried. They decide the best approach is for them to split up, too. Nick puts his arm around Winnie and they begin their search. Alex, crying hysterically, runs up to Casey and throws his arms around her.

"Casey, Jazzy ran away because of me! I said terrible things to her. I told her that nobody would ever want to adopt us because she always dresses like a tomboy. I yelled at her for throwing her ball inside the house. I didn't mean it. Casey, we gotta find her!"

"Alex, we all say things we don't mean. Everything's going to be fine and we will find her."

"I want to go with you to look for her."

"No, you and Olivia need to stay with Phyllis in case Jazzy comes back."

Still sobbing, he relents, "Well, okay."

Nick and Winnie go from storefront to storefront showing Jazzy's picture. Time and time again the storeowners shake their heads, *no*.

Casey walks through Piedmont Park yelling Jazzy's name and combing the area. She follows the path around the duck pond and shows Jazzy's picture to everyone she passes. They all shake their heads, *no*. She goes to the lemonade stand and shows Jazzy's picture. The vendor shakes his head, *no*. Casey approaches a mime and shows Jazzy's picture. *No*, he hasn't seen her.

The Odreys, Phyllis, Alex and Olivia look all around the playground equipment, in their rooms, even in their closets, calling Jazzy's name. Olivia kneels and prays by her bed, then looks under her bed. Nick and Winnie search the ball field. With his hands cupped to his eyes, Alex looks through a bay window to the outside. Harmony and Ken pause on a sidewalk so Harmony can get an update. She phones Phyllis, who reports there is still no sign of Jazzy. Casey stands by an exhibit at the Botanical Gardens showing Jazzy's picture. No one has seen her.

It's Erika Marie's debut in the Atlanta market. Patrons flock into the Georgia Dome for her concert. Normally, Casey would be there proudly supporting her artist, but this time, Jazzy takes priority. Erika Marie is approached backstage by a handsome young man wearing an ID. They've talked on several occasions and a crush has been in the making for a while. He is very charming and flirts unapologetically.

"How about we get together after the concert?"

Erika looks around for her father.

"I'll have to ask my dad."

"No you don't. I'm staying at the same hotel you are. Meet me at the pool as soon as you get back there."

The concert emcee introduces Erika Marie.

"Ladies and gentlemen, please welcome Hit Maker Music recording artist, Erika Marie!"

Erika looks at the young man, smiles shyly and goes onstage.

The hunt for Jazzy continues. After several hours of searching, Casey, exhausted and feeling defeated, finds herself unexplainably drawn to Christ Community Church. With a tear-stained face, she slips into the end of a pew close to the front of the sanctuary. She leans back in the seat and her eyes are drawn up to a stained-glass picture of Jesus holding a little lamb. Feeling uneasy, Casey turns to survey the room. She is alone. Turning back to the picture of Jesus holding the little lamb, she nervously begins to speak.

"I'm still not convinced You're really listening, or that You even exist, for that matter …"

She feels the hot tears run down her cheeks.

"… but I've met so many good people in these last months who do believe in You. Quite honestly, I would try anything to get Jazzy back. She's so little. She can't protect herself and we don't know where she is …"

In the balcony, above and behind where Casey is sitting, Jazzy, holds her Teddy bear and peeks over the balcony railing at Casey. Slowly and quietly she begins making her way down the staircase that leads to the main floor. Then she silently walks down the aisle toward Casey, who, in hopeless desperation, continues to sob.

"… so if You are real, please, help us find Jazzy. Tell us where to look. I'll do anything. Please."

Quietly, Jazzy has now made her way down to the pew where Casey sits. She stands next to Casey and gently places her hand on her shoulder.

"Casey?"

Startled, Casey jumps up out of her seat and she and Jazzy scream simultaneously. She swoops Jazzy up and begins hugging and kissing her face and squeezing her tightly.

"Where have you been? We've been so worried. Oh, thank you, God! Thank you, thank you, thank you!"

Overcome with joy, Casey continues holding a tired and quiet Jazzy. Casey gets another glimpse of the stained-glass image of Jesus holding the little lamb and deliberates the reality of its time-tested message. Finally, she looks up to the heavens, smiles and hugs Jazzy as if she will never let go.

Anxious to share the good news, Casey takes Jazzy back to the Eagle's Nest and reports that what was lost is now found. Phyllis calls everyone back to the home.

The dining table is filled with half-eaten snacks. Nick, Winnie, the Odreys, Ken, Harmony and Phyllis are still sitting at the table when Casey reenters the room from tucking in the kids.

"What a night!" Casey sighs.

"Everybody in bed?" inquires Phyllis.

"Asleep before their heads hit their pillows."

The Odreys, Harmony and Ken bid everyone farewell for the night.

"It's time for my head to hit a pillow," says Mr. Odrey.

"Good night," everyone says in unison.

Casey sits back down at the table with Winnie, Nick and Phyllis. With an open and vulnerable look at each of them, she shares a very personal epiphany.

"There's something I need to tell you guys. My community service hours were completed about a hundred hours ago. Lately, I haven't been coming here out of obligation. I've continued to come because, well, I've fallen madly in love."

Everyone listens intently.

"I've given this a great deal of thought. I want to adopt Alex, Olivia and Jazzy."

Seeing their stunned faces, tears well up in Casey's eyes.

"I'm smitten. I think about them all the time. When I'm working I can't wait for a free second to call or come by the home. I love taking them on outings and watching them experience things for the first time. When I watch their peaceful little faces as they sleep, I …"

Casey pats her heart, struggling to speak as she cries without reservation. Nick sobs too as Winnie, completely amazed by this news, hands each of them a tissue.

"Sometimes at night I look at their pictures and it brings me such, such joy. I have never felt this way about anything or anyone. I even love them more than … more than … my job."

Winnie jokingly clutches at her chest and responds, "Oh, my heavens, this *is* serious!"

"I want to be their mom!" Casey confesses. She blows her nose and wipes her tears.

Even Winnie is overcome by her comment. For as long as she can remember, Casey has had many lofty goals. But becoming a mom was never on the list.

Phyllis interjects, "I'm very pleased to hear that you feel the way you do. But after all this time of no interest in the kids, about a week ago a couple met with me and we've begun the adoption process."

"What? Well, who are they?"

"I'm sorry, that's confidential."

"Well, you have to let me put in a bid, too."

"Casey, they're not a piece of real estate," says Winnie.

"Well, I have to fight for this. I mean, is this couple willing to take all three kids? They can't be separated. It just wouldn't be right. I know we belong together and that's that. Tell me what to do."

"You mustn't say anything to the children and get their hopes up. You'll need to fill out a host of forms and I'll take it from there."

Determined, Casey replies, "Well, okay then. Sounds like a plan. Just get me what I need and I'm on it."

After a long, eventful day, Casey is ready to leave.

"I've got to run. I promised Bert I'd drop back in and see him tonight. Wait until I tell him I've decided I want kids!"

※ ※ ※

At the hospital, Casey hurries to Bert's room. She can't wait to tell him how she is taking his advice. She has decided to get her life in balance with less time at work, more time with friends and time for a family of her own. She knows he will be thrilled with her desire to become a devoted mom.

The elevator seems to move at a snail's pace. Finally, it reaches Bert's floor. Casey gets off and proceeds down the hall to his room. Through the open door, she finds all the flowers are gone and his bed is empty. She runs down the hall to the nurses' station to find out where he's been moved. The nurse on duty gently tells her that Bert quietly passed in his sleep. She bursts into tears, overcome with both shock and grief. *Why did it have to happen now?*

His words of wisdom begin to echo in her mind, reminding her that life is precious and that she must learn from his mistakes. She leaves the hospital with his last words reverberating in her heart. Once this horrible pain she is feeling finally subsides, she will be able to appreciate how fortunate she has been to have had her last conversation with him. But for now, all she can do is wish for just one more conversation to share her news with him.

Erika Marie's concert is over and she is back at the Four Seasons where undetected by Bud, she has successfully sneaked out. Erika Marie and the young man from the concert sit together on a lounge chair, poolside. They are talking, laughing and sharing a thermos containing punch with vodka. They look around to assure their privacy and quickly begin disrobing to their underwear for skinny dipping. Unknown to them, they are being photographed by paparazzi.

After a couple of days in which she's cried until she has no more tears left, Casey feels like today is the perfect day to make a well-deserved tribute. A press conference is called at Hit Maker Music where the media hover around the quadrant like a biblical-size plague. Annie, the Odreys, Winnie, Nick, Harmony and Ken mingle with the press as Casey prepares to speak. She approaches the podium holding a cardboard sign, *SLINGSHOT RECORDS*.

"As many of you are aware, Bert Elliot, my business partner since the beginning, has passed away. Recently, Bert expressed his desire for us to have a gospel label. I fought him on it. But in his honor and because I've had a change of heart, I am announcing a new gospel label to be launched at the beginning of next year. I asked my friend Harmony Jones, the choir director at the Christ Community Church what we should call it and she said she thought that *Slingshot Records* would be a good name. She told me how throughout the Bible, God used small things and ordinary people to accomplish extraordinary things."

Casey looks down at her notes.

"David was an ordinary shepherd boy who killed a giant named Goliath, using only a slingshot and a stone. Harmony says it's a reminder that little becomes much in the hands of the Lord. And just like David with his slingshot, we can all be used to accomplish great things if we take what we have and we trust God to use it."

"And so we have a new gospel label: *Slingshot Records!*"

Casey's words resonate as everyone applauds.

"I'd also like to announce that the president of Slingshot Records will be my longtime, right-hand woman, Annie Clement."

Everyone cheers!

Casey winks at a stunned and elated Annie and then offers her a personal word.

"And yes, Annie, that will come with an substantial increase in salary and benefits."

Annie fights back the tears as the crowd laughs and congratulates her with more applause.

※ ※ ※

At the Four Seasons, the newsstand has just received the evening addition of the Atlanta Journal. Bud picks up the paper and turns to the front page of the entertainment section. The headline says, "Platinum Award-Winning Role Model, Erika Marie, Caught Consuming Alcohol and Skinny Dipping."

Bud is infuriated! He feels betrayed. He quickly points out to Erika that her concert sponsors were willing to kick her to the curb because of her affiliation with Hit Maker Music and Casey Alliston, now how much more they will disassociate with her after this disaster! He is certain the conversations with new record companies interested in signing her will be end because of her actions. In fact, she may end up with no record deal at all! Erika, ashamed and broken, is crumpled in a corner of her hotel room, face buried in her hands, crying and dreading the consequences she knows will come soon.

Chapter 18

The couple that surfaced recently and has expressed interest in adopting Alex has been thoroughly checked out. They are who they claim to be and have come to the home today to be formally introduced. Phyllis introduces Alex to Mrs. Sutton, his deceased father's half sister, and her husband, and then leaves them to get acquainted.

"So, you're my half aunt?" Alex inquires.

"That's correct," responds Mrs. Sutton.

Alex gets right to the point.

"Where you been?"

"Alex, I was adopted when I was young. I never knew I had any siblings. About a year ago I started tracing my family history. That's when I found out I had a brother, and that my brother had a son. I've been looking for you ever since."

"Well there's something you should know. I have two sisters. And we have to be adopted together."

Olivia and Jazzy are listening to the conversation and try to peek around the corner.

"Really? I wasn't aware of any siblings."

"Well, you wouldn't believe how birth records can get messed up."

The Suttons listen with curiosity.

"Would you like to meet them?"

"Well of course," says Mrs. Sutton.

Alex summons the girls, who are anxiously waiting.

"Olivia! Jazzy!"

Olivia and Jazzy gleefully bounce into the room. Alex smiles proudly as Mrs. Sutton silently comprehends the situation. Mr. Sutton, not yet connecting the dots, looks slightly perplexed.

After an hour or so, Phyllis returns to check on things. For a first meeting, it seems to be going well. In fact, maybe better than well.

"How's everyone doing?" Phyllis asks.

"Fine," says Alex.

"If it's okay, we'd like to come by on Saturday and take everyone out to dinner," says Mr. Sutton.

"By everyone, do you mean me and my sisters?"

"Yes," Mrs. Sutton replies with a big smile.

"That sounds like a good plan," says Phyllis. "What time?"

"Let's say six o'clock."

The Suttons request hugs from the kids who respond wholeheartedly. As they drive off, the kids watch them from the bay window until their car is out of sight.

※※※

It's date night for Harmony and Ken, but this particular night will be one like no other, one to be remembered as long as they both shall live. Ken has gone to extreme effort to make sure every detail of this evening is perfect in every way. Dressed to the nines, they sit at a table at Babettes, an upscale French restaurant in the Highlands. They both order the chef's special that includes a hearts of palm salad, lobster bisque and rack of lamb with fingerling potatoes and sautéed spinach. For desert they enjoy a flourless chocolate cake with a scoop of rum raisin ice cream accompanied by an espresso.

As they sit chatting over empty dinner plates, a waiter removes the plates while another brings a chilled bottle of sparkling apple juice and champagne glasses. The waiter pours each of them a glass and leaves them to resume their conversation. Ken lifts his glass and proposes a toast.

"To a love that lasts forever!"

Harmony clinks her glass with his.

"Awww, that is so sweet, Ken. Yes, to everlasting love."

Ken puts down his glass and pulls out a small box from his coat pocket. He gets down on one knee and takes Harmony's hand. Her eyes widen as he opens the box and reveals a glittering engagement ring.

"Harmony Jones, will you marry me?"

Harmony responds with a resounding, "Yes! Thank you, Jesus! Yes!"

Everyone in the restaurant hears her praises and joins the celebration with wild applause. Ken raises her up from the table and kisses her for all the world to see. She holds up her ring and gives the patrons a panoramic view. This event is proof that a fervently prayed prayer has been answered by a good God who hears the requests of His children. Harmony knows it. She believes it. And she will thank Him for His faithfulness all day, every day for the rest of her life.

※※※

It's Saturday afternoon and Casey, Alex, Olivia, and Jazzy walk together eating blueberry snow cones in Piedmont Park. Alex is consumed with questions and intent on analyzing them until he uproots answers that satisfy his inquiring mind.

"If my aunt and uncle won't adopt all of us, I'm not going with them," Alex resolves.

Smiling with very blue lips, Jazzy and Olivia nod their heads in agreement. As difficult as it is for Casey to be unbiased and diplomatic, she gives it her best shot.

"Well sweetie, don't worry about that right now. None of us can ever have too many friends or relatives. You're glad you've met them, aren't you?"

Timid to press his opinion, Alex shrugs his shoulders.

"Well, give them a chance. Whether they adopt you or not, give them a chance. They're part of your family."

Looking straight ahead and without acknowledging Casey's comment, Alex continues walking. In good humor, she nudges him.

"Hey, you."

Alex looks up at her.

"Give them a chance, okay?"

Reluctantly he monotones, "Okay."

※※※

Phyllis sits with the Suttons in the living room of the Eagle's Nest, awaiting the return of Casey and the kids.

"We've been trying to have a baby for ten years. We've tried everything," Mrs. Sutton shares.

"We see finding Alex as a perfect solution to finally having a family," Mr. Sutton adds.

"I can appreciate that," Phyllis comments.

"Even if the adoption is denied, couldn't Alex be awarded to us anyway?" Mrs. Sutton asks.

"We've established that my wife is his blood relative," adds Mr. Sutton.

"Let's just take it a step at a time and see what happens. Right now it's important for you to get to know each other."

The front door opens and the conversation between the Suttons and Phyllis is temporarily suspended as Casey and the kids enter, chatting happily. Their chatter stops and they warily turn to the Suttons. Phyllis breaks the sudden silence.

"Hello everyone! Looks like you've had an enjoyable afternoon!"

"We always have fun with Casey," Jazzy says as she hugs Casey around her legs.

"That's wonderful! Alex as you can see, your aunt and uncle have come to take you and the girls to dinner."

"Coooooool," says Jazzy.

"Please go change your clothes," says Phyllis.

The kids comply and Phyllis makes introductions. "Casey, I'd like for you to meet Alex's aunt and uncle, Mr. and Mrs. Sutton."

They shake hands.

"Nice to meet you. It must be quite rewarding to be a volunteer," Mrs. Sutton says.

Phyllis gives Casey a look that indicates a plea for self control.

"Yes. It is."

"Do you have children of your own?" asks Mr. Sutton.

"No, but I've just recently applied for adoption."

"That's wonderful! Are you trying to adopt a boy or a girl?"

Phyllis holds her breath, hoping Casey will show restraint.

"Either. I'd actually be fine with either."

Alex, Olivia, and Jazzy return in their dress clothes. Casey bends down to say goodbye and gives each one a warm hug.

"Have a nice dinner, kids. Use your best table manners."

"The first time we went out to eat with Casey she told us we ate like Vikings!" exclaims Alex.

Slightly embarrassed, Olivia and Jazzy giggle.

"So she taught us how to eat nice," Jazzy explains.

"That's good! Well, are we ready?" asks Mrs. Sutton.

"Bye, Casey," the kids say in unison.

"Nice meeting you, Casey," smiles Mrs. Sutton.

"Nice meeting you, too," Casey politely replies as she walks out the door.

🍋🍋🍋

Grecco's is crowded but their reserved table is waiting. The smell of garlic bread permeates the air. The Suttons help the kids tie bibs around their necks. Seated around a large round table, they order generous portions of spaghetti for everyone. Mr. Sutton notices Jazzy struggling with the pasta. He reaches over and cuts it up for her. Jazzy pats his wrist and their eyes meet.

"You showed up just in time!"

Mrs. Sutton looks on adoringly. She notices Olivia having the same difficulty and offers assistance. Olivia smiles at her and responds shyly.

"Thank you."

"You have such nice manners."

"Casey taught us," Alex smiles.

Not too long after attempting to consume a very large dessert, Jazzy is asleep in Mr. Sutton's lap with the half-eaten sundae left in front of her. Olivia is sitting on Mrs. Sutton's lap. She carefully wipes her mouth with her napkin, and then kisses Mrs. Sutton on the cheek. Mrs. Sutton holds her a little tighter. Happy to observe their interaction, Alex enjoys finishing his dessert.

🍋🍋🍋

Casey is engrossed in her longtime love for recording. She sits at the soundboard of the Hit Maker Music recording studio next to the sound engineer, as the introduction to the song "Thankful" plays. Harmony, wearing a headset, stands at a microphone inside the vocal booth. Winnie, Nick, Ken and the Odreys sit on couches behind Casey. The engineer cues Harmony to begin singing.

"Comin' acha."

Harmony begins singing the song but quickly bursts into tears. Casey looks concerned. The engineer stops the track and Casey hits the talkback button.

"Harmony, what's the matter?"

Ken stands up and waits for her response as Harmony tries to compose herself.

"I'm fine. It's just that for my whole life I've dreamed of two things: Getting married ..."

Harmony looks at her engagement ring, blows a kiss to Ken and then continues. "... and recording a record." She wipes her tears. "Both my dreams are coming true. And I'm about to sing a song titled 'Thankful.' God is so good to me and I really am thankful."

"Then sing it to me exactly from that place, Harmony. Comin' acha."

Casey nods to the engineer to start the track. Harmony closes her eyes as though singing directly to God and sings "Thankful."

When she has finished, Casey waves her into the control room where they listen to the recording. The entire gang congratulates her on the superb vocal performance as Casey pulls out a wrapped gift from under the console.

"Okay, gentlemen. You'll need to leave us for a moment."

Ken, Nick and Mr. Odrey leave the girlfriends to themselves. Winnie and Mrs. Odrey gather around Casey as she hands the gift to Harmony.

"Sorry I couldn't make it to your wedding shower. A little something for the honeymoon."

Harmony opens the gift and holds up several sexy nightgowns. "Oooooh, girl! My goodness! These are beautiful! Can't wait to wear them!"

"Wear them well, soon-to-be Mrs. Odrey. And have a great rest of the evening! I have an after-hours meeting down the hall I need to get to."

Casey walks down the hall into her office. There sitting quietly across from her desk, Bud and Erika Marie await her arrival. Annie keeps them company and acts as a witness and minutes keeper for the upcoming discussion. Bud is resolved to be humble.

"Casey, would you take us back?"

"Bud, as far as I'm concerned, you never left."

"And you can say anything you want to this rebellious, shameful child of mine!"

"I would say to her what I would say to you. Everyone makes mistakes and everyone deserves a second chance."

He nods affirmatively. Erika jumps up from her chair, rounds the desk and embraces Casey. With her tear-stained face and her head buried in Casey's shoulder, Erika whispers, "I'm so sorry! Thank you, Casey."

Chapter 19

A month has passed since Casey and the Suttons turned in their paperwork for adopting Alex, Olivia and Jazzy. Phyllis sits behind a desk piled to the ceiling with paperwork, as she talks on the phone and thumbs through an open folder.

"Yes, I understand. Thank you."

She hangs up the phone and looks up to see Winnie knocking on her open door.

"Any word?"

Phyllis looks solemn.

"Yes. The board approved the Suttons' adoption of all three kids. I need to make the calls to them and to Casey."

"Let me tell Casey."

Immediately, Winnie sets out for Casey's high rise. Casey answers her door to find a very melancholy Winnie.

"I didn't get them did I?"

Winnie shakes her head, no.

Casey's eyes fill with tears. Winnie gives her a long, empathetic hug and they wander into the kitchen. Casey busies herself with making lattes and they take their mugs into the living room.

"I'm so sorry things didn't turn out the way we had hoped."

"Me, too."

"I know it's hard to see right now but eventually I know you'll be able to look back and understand why things went the way they did."

"The Suttons will be great parents. There's no doubt about that."

Choking back tears, Winnie nods in agreement. Casey can't hold back her tears.

"I am coming away with something: I have learned how it feels to love, totally and with complete abandon. I've never felt that way before about anything or anyone. What's most important is that they get adopted and have the chance to be part of a family."

"And that's what pure love is: unselfishly wanting the best for the ones you love. And you're doing that."

After a long pause, Winnie continues.

"Are you going to go over to the Eagle's Nest when the Suttons come pick them up—to congratulate them?"

"Hadn't thought about it, but I probably should. Maybe I can give them a framed picture of us or make them an official *I'm your Auntie* certificate. I don't know, what do you think? How about vouchers for outings with me?"

Winnie laughs. "I think all those ideas are great! They're supposed to be there at 11:00 a.m. tomorrow to pick up the kids."

"Okay."

Winnie says goodbye and Casey goes to work on her arts and crafts for the kids. Phyllis calls the Suttons and catches them just as they are leaving a doctor's appointment. Phyllis tells them the news and they respond by giving her some news of their own. They are jubilant.

After speaking to the Suttons, Phyllis decides to call Casey, who is in her sunroom busily making the kids their surprise gifts. Casey answers the phone and stoically listens to Phyllis. Casey hangs up, picks up a framed picture of the kids and begins to cry. She never remembers crying this much, and she feels worn out, so she decides to go to bed early tonight. Tomorrow will be a life-changing day, one that she and the kids will always remember.

※ ※ ※

Casey rises early. She packs up her gifts in a tote bag, grabs her triple latte and sunglasses, and then leaves for a long, early-morning walk to the Eagle's Nest.

She cuts through Piedmont Park and passes a lemonade vendor with a sign on the cart that says, *When Life Gives You Lemons, Make Lemonade.*

As she walks, she remembers many occasions in this park she has enjoyed with the children. The memories make her heart overflow with gratefulness. Tears of joy begin trickling down her cheeks. She brushes them away and adjusts her sunglasses.

Finally, she reaches the Christ Community Church. She tosses her coffee cup just outside and then quietly enters the sanctuary. Slowly, walking down the center aisle to the front, her eyes rest on the stained glass where Jesus holds the little lamb. She sits on the front pew and continues to reminisce about her experiences in church and at the Eagle's Nest with Alex, Olivia and Jazzy.

Casey remembers coming into this sanctuary for the first time and meeting Jazzy, Olivia and Alex. She recalls her first trip with them to the bookstore, when Jazzy taught her the proper way to read using varied character voices. Casey smiles. She remembers playing baseball with the kids and the time that Jazzy burned one into her glove.

She sat right here when she came to support Alex in his first solo. And a few weeks later, she heard Olivia's first words after the ballet at the Fox. Then there was Jazzy's confession of making a wish when Olivia blew out her birthday candles, wishing that Casey would be her mommy.

※ ※ ※

Next door inside the Eagle's Nest, Phyllis, Alex, Olivia and Jazzy sit together on the couch. Phyllis gives some instructions. The kids listen intently. When she has finished her directions, the Odreys, Nick, Winnie, Harmony, Ken and Phyllis help the children pack.

Nick ties Alex's tie and Mr. Odrey helps him put on his jacket. Winnie puts the finishing touches on Jazzy's hair with a bow, and tries to keep her from itching herself in her lacy dress. Phyllis buttons the back of Olivia's dress. Mrs. Odrey admires the girls' good looks.

※ ※ ※

Still sitting in the sanctuary, Casey recalls when she and Jazzy flew to see a real lighthouse and how Jazzy made her own birthday wish, again, for Casey to be her mommy.

Casey removes her sunglasses and wipes away a tear. She pans the stained glass one last time and recounts the day Jazzy went missing. It was right here Jazzy tapped her on the shoulder to make herself known and Casey swooped her up to plaster her with hugs and kisses. Yes, that was the day she first realized all of her walls had fallen to dust. She realized what it is to have an opened heart, with an unlimited capacity to love. Contented, she slowly fills her lungs with air, then exhales and stands.

Still a bit pensive, she glances upward one last time at Jesus holding the little lamb. She smiles and walks over to the Eagle's Nest.

Phyllis, the Odreys, Winnie and Nick give the kids, who are dressed in their Sunday best, one last pep talk. Phyllis addresses the children.

"Well, this is the day you've been waiting for. We're going to walk together down the hallway and go through the double doors. Your new family will be waiting for you on the other side."

With suitcases in tow, Alex, Olivia and Jazzy start down the corridor with Nick and Winnie in the lead and the rest of the adults to their rear. Their faces say it all: a mixture of excitement and a slight fear of all that is to come. Today, they will leave the familiar place they've called home for so long, to embark on the unknown, with all of the wonder, unanswered questions and anticipated dreams come true.

Jazzy is fidgety in her itchy dress. She'd much prefer her jeans, a T-shirt and a baseball cap, but Phyllis insisted. They are almost there. Nick and Winnie, on opposite sides of the hallway, push open the swinging double doors to the family room. The children walk through.

The Suttons stand next to each other, smiling. The kids look puzzled as Mr. Sutton touches Mrs. Sutton's tummy.

"Hi kids. We have some great news to share with you. Yesterday we found out that we are expecting ... triplets! So we've decided it would be best if we just remain very involved in all of your lives but as your aunt and uncle."

The kids are confused and disgruntled. They look to the other adults, who reflect the same emotions. Except Phyllis, who is having great difficulty containing her elation.

Alex asks with disappointment, "So we're not being adopted now?"

As though parting the Red Sea, the Suttons step away from each other and reveal Casey, sitting on the couch behind them. With arms outstretched and her face in a mixture of joy and tears, she stands to welcome them. They run into her arms, full speed ahead.

"You're adopting us, Casey?" Alex asks.

"I am. I did. I have!"

"All of us?" he asks.

Jazzy awaits the answer.

"You bet!"

As soon as Jazzy hears this confirmation, she opens her tiny suitcase. She takes out a T-shirt, jeans and Reeboks and begins disrobing and redressing. The love-fest continues as the celebration is moved into the dining room.

The dining room is decorated with balloons and banners. A large table full of good food has been prepared for them. Casey presents each child with framed picture of one of their special events. She explains that they can put it in their new bedrooms.

After an hour or so, the remnants of several large pizzas, a big punch bowl almost emptied of lemonade and a partially-eaten cake are left on the table. A few balloons and streamers linger. The Suttons, Nick, Winnie, the Odreys, Ken, Harmony, Phyllis, Casey, Alex, Olivia and Jazzy have enjoyed a great celebration. Jazzy sits in Casey's lap drinking lemonade.

"Well my wonderful son and daughters, I think we'd better be going home."

"Home. Sounds so nice," repeats Alex. "God answered my prayer!"

Jazzy whispers something to Olivia. Olivia shrugs her shoulders. Alex notices there's a question that needs the wisdom of a big brother.

"Jazzy, you need help with something?"

Jazzy, Olivia and Alex form a huddle. Jazzy whispers something to Alex. Casey looks concerned.

"What is it, Alex?"

"Well, Jazzy was wondering, actually we were all wondering, if, well … if it would be okay …"

"Yes?"

"We were wondering if it's okay if we call you Mom?"

The celebration ends in a waterfall of joyous tears. Casey would be called Mom from that moment on.

Chapter 20

The marquee in front of the Christ Community Church proudly announces, *Congratulations, Harmony and Ken!* A decorated limo waits out front. The doors are still open wide as few last-minute guests enter the building. The Odreys begin the procession as they are seated in their place of honor.

Ken stands at the front of the church beside the pastor. Casey, Winnie, Nick, the Suttons and Phyllis sit together in a pew. A hush comes over the auditorium. "Cannon in G" begins. Dressed in a light pink dress, Olivia comes down the aisle tossing rose petals. Behind her, Jazzy, dressed in a light pink girly tux, throws her petals as if she was throwing baseballs. Alex, in a white tux, carefully walks down the aisle carrying the rings.

"Wedding March" begins to play. The congregation stands and turns to face the back of the church. Harmony, in her wedding gown, waltzes down the aisle without an escort. Harmony reaches Ken and gives him a hug before she grasps his arm.

"Who gives this woman to be wed to this man?" asks Pastor John.

"I give myself to this wonderful man, in the mighty name of Jesus! Hallelujah! Can somebody say Amen?"

The congregation gives a hardy, "Amen!"

Pastor John says, "Harmony has a song to sing to you, Ken."

Harmony steps to the microphone and sings, "This Heart of Mine is Yours." Ken cries through the entire song. In fact, few eyes are dry when the song concludes. Harmony steps down from the stage, hugs the Odreys and then returns to stand arm in arm with Ken.

Pastor John continues and completes the nuptials.

"I now pronounce you man and wife."

Harmony squeezes Ken's arm and they gaze longingly at each other as she dabs the tears streaming down both of their faces.

"And yes, sir, you may kiss your bride!"

They seal their God-ordained covenant with a passionate kiss. They turn to face their guests, and then proceed together out of the sanctuary. After the recessional, they return for pictures. Once the photos have been taken, they join their guests outside in the large reception tent set up for their continued celebration.

It seems the entire church is in attendance. The reception is elegant, yet simple. They enjoy a beautiful array of food, socialize with many friends and well-wishers who offer toasts to their happiness. They cut their cake and laugh as each feeds the other a messy bite. When Ken throws Harmony's garter, Nick catches it. Winnie smiles with delight. The eligible young women assemble and vie for position before Harmony throws her bouquet. They all scramble, and Winnie catches the bouquet! Nick gives her a big kiss. The kids giggle and eat more cake.

Finally, Harmony and Ken get ready to make their exit. Everyone stands together in a human walkway and blows bubbles. Ken and Harmony run the gauntlet of bubbles to the limo, where the chauffeur opens the door for them to get in. As the limo pulls away, everyone waves and cheers. Harmony can't resist standing up, peering out of the sunroof and blowing kisses to everyone. She is still blowing kisses as the limo turns a corner and disappears out of sight.

Casey savors the last moments of this special celebration. She catches a glimpse of Winnie and Nick walking arm in arm to his car as Winnie smells the flowers in the bride's bouquet. The Suttons hug each of the kids, wave to Casey and get into their car. Phyllis gathers the children from the Eagle's Nest and the Odreys assist her by holding the hands of several children as they return to the home.

Casey calls to Alex, Olivia and Jazzy. They all pile into her T-Bird and drive together to their collective destination: home.

※ ※ ※

Three months have passed. Casey and the kids are at Piedmont Park walking their golden retriever and playing Frisbee. Several people in orange suits and armed with pooper-scoopers fan out over the lawn. Large rolling garbage containers announce in large green letters that *The Pooper Scooper Brigade* is here, and pet owners go to dispose of their wrappings.

Casey, with the kids and dog in tow, approach a female worker wearing dark glasses, a tennis hat and garden gloves as another woman, dressed in designer clothes, confronts the same worker.

"We expect your resignation today."

"But, surely …"

Before the worker's sentence can be completed, the woman exits in a huff, leaving the worker in tears. To her surprise, Casey recognizes the worker is Ruth Bayslow.

"Ruth?"

Still sniffling, Ruth responds.

"I have to resign as president of my garden club. My Fifi pottied on the sidewalk in front of my townhouse and I was sentenced to twenty community service hours. I was arrested for littering! I feel so, so …"

Casey places her wrapped poop into Ruth's container, puts her arm around Ruth and consoles her.

"Dumped on?" Casey says in an effort to help her complete her sentence.

Stephen, Ruth's widower son, a handsome, distinguished man in his early forties who is accompanied by two small children, approaches Casey and Ruth from behind. He playfully addresses his mom.

"How's my favorite convict?"

Casey and Ruth turn toward the voice simultaneously and look like the cat that ate the canary. Ruth reacts.

"You're not at all amusing, Stephen."

A big tease, he continues relentlessly, winking at Casey. "We're here to spring you for lunch!"

Ruth unzips her orange suit and begins to step out of it. Stephen and Casey smile at each other as Ruth makes the introductions.

"Casey this is my son, Stephen, and his children, Lily and Max, ages six and four."

"Hello, nice to finally meet you, all of you. And these are my children, Alex, Olivia and Jazzy."

Alex shakes hands with Stephen as Jazzy and Olivia give high fives to Lily and Max. Casey and Stephen smile broadly and find an immediate connection. They chat a bit more before parting ways for the lunch date with Ruth.

"May I call you sometime?"

"Sure, your mom has the number."

The kids giggle amongst themselves as they all part ways. Casey and her kids continue walking through the park. High above an adjacent road, they see a billboard advertising Harmony and the Christ Community Choir. Casey smiles proudly and flips on her iPod just in time to hear the DJ make a monumental announcement.

"And as of this morning's Billboard chart, the #1 gospel record in the country is Harmony Jones Odrey and the Christ Community Church Choir singing, 'I Will Rejoice.'"

The song begins to play and the kids sing along as they continue walking. Alex waves his arms as though conducting the choir. A mime approaches and hands Jazzy a balloon. Jazzy hands it to Casey who walks with it briefly, remembering a day not so long ago when this same thing had happened. She had taken a balloon from a mime on the day she was forced out of her company. That was the worst day of her life, and she knew her life would never be the same. Smiling, she knew she had been right, but not in the way she had expected. Casey has a question for the kids.

"Let it go or hold onto it?"

Jumping up and down, they say in unison, "Let it go, Mom. Let it go!"

"Yeah if you don't let it go, we'll never know how high it can fly," says Alex.

Casey smiles and pauses on the wisdom in his innocent statement.

"Okay, here goes!"

Casey releases the balloon. They all watch as it soars higher and higher, freely unrestrained, without interference, climbing into the heavens.

They continue walking until they reach the lemonade stand Casey has passed a million times before. She buys everyone a glass and smiles when for the first time she actually contemplates the slogan on side of the stand, *When Life Gives You Lemons, Make Lemonade.* Adoringly, she watches Alex, Olivia and Jazzy consume their lemonade with unbridled gusto. However, she willfully sips hers slowly and drinks in the beautiful picture before her of her three children.

Casey assumes her role as a mom like she was born for it. Hit Maker Music continues to flourish, particularly the gospel music division. She and the children attend the Christ Community Church every week and desiring to learn and understand more about God, she has just enrolled in her first Beth Moore Women's Bible study, titled *Breaking Free*. (With all the challenges she's faced these last few months she was drawn by the title.) They frequently volunteer as a family at the Eagle's Nest, serving in any capacity that helps the residents. Casey and Stephen have been group-dating with all the kids and that seems to be developing nicely.

The children grow by leaps and bounds, flourishing in every sense of the word. They are all doing well in school. Alex won the Young Citizen Award, loves singing in the youth choir and continues to make the honor roll. Jazzy is the shortstop for the Pony League T-ball team, enjoys learning to read and gets very high marks in art class. Olivia enjoys Spanish class and writing poems. She dances with the grace of a gazelle, although she continues to be cited by all her teachers for talking too much.

Through her life journey so far, Casey has become convinced of a few things: There has to be a God, not maybe, not possibly but definitely; and it is His plan that we all can know Him personally. Life may be filled with challenges, twists and turns, but all roads lead to Him. She has also concluded that there is purpose in everything, the good, the bad and the ugly; the lessons earned, lessons burned and lessons learned.

And finally, even when we go through things we don't understand, we can trust the God who not only sees the big picture, He painted it. And therefore we can be confident in knowing that when life gives us lemons, we can, in fact make lemonade. And Casey will be the first to tell you that for her, it is a tall, cool, thirst-quenching glass, indeed.

Acknowledgements

Always first and foremost, I would like to thank my Lord and Savior Jesus Christ. Simply put I am a sinner and, but for Jesus, without a means of forgiveness. No amount of good deeds or good works could adequately settle my sin debt. The Bible says that the penalty for my sin is death and spending eternity apart from God.

However, Jesus gave His life for me and died in my place. By accepting what He did on the cross on my behalf and by placing my trust and belief in this substitutionary great exchange, my sin has been forgiven, my offenses toward a Holy God erased and my relationship with God fully restored.

"For God loved the world so much that He gave His one and only Son, so that everyone who believes in Him will not perish but have eternal life. God sent his Son into the world not to judge the world, but to save the world through Him. John 3:16-17 (New Living Translation)

I know with all certainty that when I draw my last breath here on earth, I will be welcomed into heaven for all eternity, having nothing to do with anything I did but only because of what He was willing to do on my behalf! Thank you, Jesus!

I'd like to thank the love of my life, my wonderful husband, Jim. With you, life is such a great adventure! You're the best husband on the planet! Thank you for all the encouragement and support you give to this writer-wife. "This Heart of Mine is Yours." (Hey, that would make a good song! ☺ I love you so much!

I'd like to thank my children and their spouses, Merry, Dean, Jaimee, Jonathan and Katie for making me feel loved, welcomed and so much a part of this family. I love being a mom without labor pains! To my grands, Alex, Springer, Humza, Ameenah, Azaan, Coen and Zain: all of you have brought more joy and love into my life than I ever knew possible. I love you, *MORE!* ☺

To my mommy, Callie M. Douglas, who at eighty-seven years old still volunteers twice a week at the hospital, bakes muffins for her coworkers, mails out bulletins and birthday cards for her church and helps teachers at an elementary school. A life spent in service to others. What an inspiration! I love you, Mommy!

To my bee-keeping Poppie; my sister, the most generous, thoughtful person I know, Diann; her amazing hubby, Dave; my incredible brother, Rick; my hilarious niece Erika; and my nephew, the bomb musician Austin: I love you, *huge!*

To Bab: who'd have thought that meeting over a mound of cantaloupe would have resulted in a thirty-year friendship and songwriting team that's still going strong! I love you, suga!

To Paula: only God knows how many precious babies have been born because of your dedication to crisis pregnancy and homes for unwed mothers. You're an inspiration to watch as you pour your life out in service to the Lord and to those who desperately need to know His love. Continue to " follow the Ancient Paths and your way will be made well!"

To my girlies, Katrina, Michele, Janee, Beth, Lynda, Helen and Paula: for the friendship, the sista-hood, the fellowship for the journey, the lunches, the cry-fests, the laughter-fests, the Bible studies, all the teas, the beach and the cheering section at my wedding! What would I do without you?

To Kiki, Wendy, Kathleen, Sherry, Kim, Holly, Gin, Rob, Steph, and Joanne: thank you for your friendship, love, support and encouragement. Also, could never have walked down the aisle without your help and one amazing bridal shower!

To Dr. Jules, my friend and editor extraordinaire: thank you for your expertise and for being a High C! ☺

To Dorian: thank you for lending your gifts and talents to my book cover and websites.

And lastly, to children everywhere: may you know that before God ever hung the first star He knew you and that you would be born in this place and at this time. He uniquely fashioned you with His own hands. He has a grand purpose and plan for your life. You are valuable because the God of the universe, your Heavenly Father says so. You are special because there is no one else designed to look like you like and to be able to do what only you can do. Be reminded every moment of every day, that you are a priceless treasure, indeed!

※ ※ ※

Suggestions for Becoming Involved in Helping Distressed and At-Risk Children

Faithbridge Foster Care: www.faithbridgefostercare.org

Dave Thomas Foundation: www.davethomasfoundation.org

The Living Vine: www.thelivingvine.org

Chiang Rai Children's Home-(Thailand): www.asiaslittleones.org

Mercy Ministries: www.mercyministries.org

Jubilee City: http://jubileecityug.org/JubileeKids/his_kids.php

CASA, Court Appointed Special Advocates for Children: www.casacis.org

The Radiance Foundation: www.theradiancefoundation.org

Paul Anderson Youth Home: www.payh.org

Sally's Lambs: www.sallyslambs.org

Calvary Kids: www.calvarykids.org

Eagle Ranch: www.eagleranch.org

Goshen Valley Boys Ranch: www.goshenvalley.org

Big Oak Ranch: www.bigoak.org

Connect with Me Online:

Please visit my website: www.donnadhere.com

Follow Donna D on: twitter@donnadhere

www.facebook.com/MakeLemonadethebook

For booking information contact: stacy@therobinsonagency.com